The Mystery Fancier

Jan·Feb 1984 $3

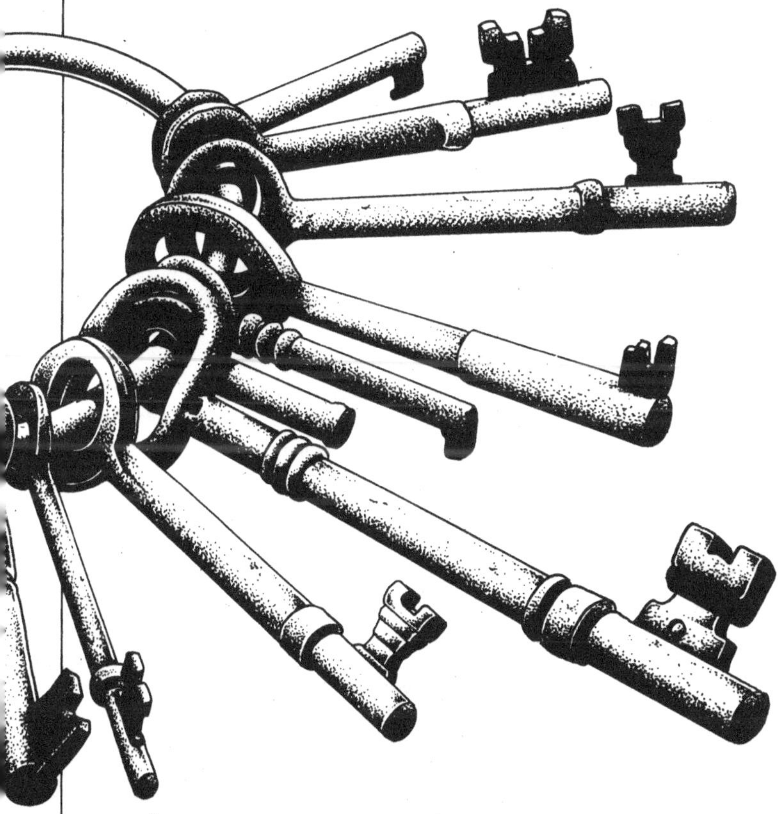

©brad w foster·1984

The Mystery Fancier

Volume 8, Number 1
January/February 1984

TABLE OF CONTENTS

MYSTERIOUSLY SPEAKING	Page 1
The Murder Cases of Pinklin West By Robert Sampson	Page 3
The Dr. Davie Novels of V.C. Clinton-Baddeley By Earl F. Bargainnier	Page 8
Can We Reach Agreement? By J.R. Christopher	Page 14
IT'S ABOUT CRIME By Marvin Lachman	Page 16
REEL MURDERS Movie Reviews by Walter Albert	Page 23
VERDICTS Book Reviews	Page 26
THE DOCUMENTS IN THE CASE Letters	Page 38

The Mystery Fancier
(USPS:428-590)

Stephen A. Stilwell, Editor
3004 E. 25th Street
Minneapolis, MN 55406

Guy M. Townsend, Publisher
(and Eminence Grise)
1711 Clifty Drive
Madison, IN 47250

SUBSCRIPTION RATES: Second-class mail, U.S. and Canada, $15.00 per year (6 issues); first-class mail, U.S. and Canada, $18.00; overseas surface mail, $15.00; overseas air mail, $21.00. Overseas subscribers please pay in international money order, check drawn on U.S. bank, or currency; no checks drawn on foreign banks, please. Direct correspondence and manuscripts to the editor; subscription payments and problems should be directed to the publisher.

Single copy price: $3.00
Second-class postage paid at Madison, Indiana
Copyright 1984 by Guy M. Townsend
All rights reserved for contributors
ISSN:0146-3160

Covers by Brad W. Foster

First, I'd like to apologize for the lateness of this issue. It is, of course, the fault of the eminence grise. It's going to be real nice to be able to blame the problems that arise of someone else. (Sorry Guy). Actually, there are a couple of reasons for the delay, though they are related. The transfer of the computer took a little longer than expected because we needed to be sure that the two were compatible, so it arrived only a short time (like two days) before the birth of my second daughter. So I had a little less time than expected to familiarize myself with the machine before I had to get back into fatherhood. My other daughter is three and a half and requires much less attention than Laura, the new one. Things have eased a bit so I hope to get this, and all future issues out without further delays. He said jokingly. We shall see.

A little bit about myself. I'm nearly middle-aged, have a lovely wife and two lovely daughters, ages 3 1/2 and 5 weeks. I work full-time in retailing (as a credit manager) and have a mystery bookstore on the side. Most, if not all, the books reviewed in the magazine will be available through me. If Otto can do it so can I. Don't hesitate to send me your want lists or new book orders and I'll do the best I can to oblige with said books.

For instance, the most important book to be published recently is the updated, expanded version of the **BIBLIOGRAPHY OF CRIME FICTION** by Allen J. Hubin. It just so happens that I have copies signed copies available. This is a book that should be on every mystery collector's shelf. Now expanded to include titles published through 1980 and with a series character chronology **and** a settings index with over 350 geographical and non-geographical locations. An invaluable reference. Published by Garland at $75.00.

There will be no more advertisements, at least until further notice.

This machine doesn't like me. I just finished telling you about all the great things happening in the field and when I told the machine to save it, it spit at me. So I'll try again with a somewhat shorter version.

The Mysterious Press has greatly expanded its publishing line for 1984 with upwards of 20 books scheduled for publication this year. Though I don't know all the details I do know that they have new books scheduled by Don Westlake, Teri White, James Ellroy, Greg Mcdonald, Walter Gibson, a collaboration between Bill Pronzini and John Lutz, the first book edition of two Shadow novelettes, a new James Cain, and a collection of Mickey Spillane short stories. They are also planning a series of paperback reprints of people like Stuart Kaminsky and Ed McBain. This is all very good news because if The Mysterious Press is healthy, so is the mystery field as a whole.

Countryman Press and Carroll & Graf are also doing good things. Countryman has brought back into print the first two "Nameless" detective novels by Bill Pronzini, as well as Lawrence Block's first hardcover novel, **After the First Death**, and Block's first two Chip Harrison books, **No Score** and **Chip Harrison Scores Again**. Though the last two are non-mysteries it is still nice to have them available. Carroll & Graf have already done us one great service by bringing back Howard Haycraft's **The Art of the Mystery Story** and are planning to publish as well his **Murder for Pleasure**, due in August. They are also doing some fine paperback reprints of people like Thomas Dewey, A.E.W. Mason, and Christianna Brand. Let's support these people and keep them active.

That is about all I have for now. Most of the review copies and stuff continue to go to GMT, so I am a little less on top of things than I'd like to be, but that should change once we get an issue out under my stewardship.

It will be apparent from this issue that I intend, at least initially, to take a somewhat lighter editorial hand than did Guy. For a couple of reasons. One, I'm less sure of myself in matters of syntax, grammar, and style than he is (as well as being less of a purist in some matters) and feel slightly uncomfortable mucking with the copy of people that I've read and enjoyed for many years. But that could change. And second, everyone has an individual style and I have no interest in making them all read alike.

The only other editorial change I have made is to stop printing the addresses of people after their letters of comment. I wish to encourage as much discussion as possible within the pages of the magazine and the printing of addresses doesn't help. I will, however, bow to the wishes of the readership and if I get a lot of flack about it, I'm willing to change. Of course, I would always be willing to forward a letter if anyone so desired. Let me hear from you on this.

I expect there will be some glitches when Guy goes to print this issue but I hope they won't be too many or too major and this reaches you without anymore delay. I trust and hope that we can be back on schedule by the end of June, but I need material, particularly articles and letters.

As always, this is your magazine and if you see something you don't like don't hesitate to let me know. I need and encourage your feedback. This is a major step in the history of TMF and I hope that I'm up to the task. There is no way that I can replace Guy (nor would I want to), but together we can keep the magazine healthy and well in his absence. (Note I did not say wealthy). Let's do it.

The Murder Cases of Pinklin West

Robert Sampson

Success isn't nearly as easy as it looks.
The 1920's mystery magazines glitter with series characters who are smiling, popular, successful, adored by readers, and sought by editors. Most have since faded to footnotes. But in their day, the wonder was in them, their light brilliant.
The wonder and the brilliance conceal a few gray facts. For every successful series character, a dozen or more others appeared and plodded and vanished. Their series were brief. Their lights burned low, even with the wick turned up.
We remember Race Williams and maybe Madame Storey. But few among us can recall Reverend Brace, who would have been a detective if the ministry hadn't called. Who remembers the ghost of Diogenes, a 2000 year old sorehead who became the chief investigator for a private detective agency? Or Nan Russell, a chorus girl become the dearest sweetest investigatrix you ever met, the adorable thing.
Or, for that matter, who recalls the bland Pinklin West?
West was one of those players who strutted and fretted his hour upon the stage of **Detective Story Magazine**, and then was heard no more. A brief candle, you might say. Six stories published during 1922-1923. Then gone.
Six stories was the usual length of a series showing promise but which, for various reasons, failed to catch on. **Detective Story** was packed with such short runs, among them Tiptoe Tatterton, Rev. Brace, Initiating Noggins, Boston Betty, and Old Windmills. They came. And very soon they went. Mostly they went.
Whatever cut them short, it did not seem to be the lack of an interested readership. In 1922, detective stories intertwined through many of the slick magazines and most of the general pulps. If you were an insatiable reader, you could also turn to the specialized mystery magazines, four of them available that year--**Black Mask, Detective Tales, Mystery**, and **Detective Story Magazine**.
Of these, **Detective Story** was still the major magazine. Founded in 1915, it had finally shaken off its dime novel origins. Now, a 144 page double-columned pulp, it offered an everchanging mixture of detectives, criminal heroes, plain crooks, and costumed bent heroes--in serial, short story, and novelette, offered each week, every week of the year, fifteen cents the copy. Nine or ten pieces of fiction were provided each issue. This in addition to two articles, five departments, and a gang of short paragraphs about crime, detectives, and criminals, used as filler in the magazine. Each paragraph was listed on the magazine's contents page, giving the impression of unbearable reading riches.
So much for the 1922 environment in which Mr. West appeared.

Mr. West, himself, is a criminologist, that favored profession of the early 1920's. Exactly what a criminologist did back then is not clear. There seems no difference between a criminologist and a private investigator. Except that the criminologist wears clean underwear.

West performs his miracles in Chicago. He and his assistant live in an apartment house in a fourth-floor suite used impartially as living quarters, office, and laboratory. At this period, all criminologists operated personal laboratories. It was because of the benign example of Craig Kennedy, who still towered high, inspiring detective story writers—as did the word rates Arthur B. Reeve received for the Kennedy adventures.

As in the Kennedy series, West's cases are told by a first-person narrator. And, like the Kennedy series, the narrator is an eager boob who could overlook a mouse in his milk.

Thorne Miller is his name. All stories are signed Thorne Miller, adding still another pseudonym to those swarming on the **Detective Story** contents page.

Miller's fictional function is to answer the telephone, saying "Pinklin West's assistant speaking." He also speculates about stray facts, draws foolish conclusions, and gives the reader someone to feel superior to. Why must West associate with such a dolt is never explained; Miller must be a poor relation.

As a curious—and likely inadvertent—consequence, Miller becomes the most vivid character of the series. Even when self-pictured as an inane babbler, he makes West look transparent.

Not that West would throw much shadow in full sunlight. You never saw such a self-effacing fellow.

Pinklin West's impassive face, his colorless, blinking eyes, certainly give no hint of his tremendous brain power, his almost uncanny ability to see things which remain hidden from the average eyes.

He also has the uncanny ability to listen. Through most of a case, he merely stands there, mild, blank faced, eyes blinking. If his eyes blink rapidly, that signals he has heard an interesting fact.

I will say that [West] is the most accomplished listener I have ever known; I have seen him listen for more than an hour without being tempted to utter so much as one syllable. Which does not mean, however, that he is an uninteresting talker when he is moved to speech, for he is fluently versed on many subjects.

You modern readers, in all your smug righteousness, may not be impressed by West. But the Chicago police certainly were. When they are stumped, West is the first man they call in. That happens less than twice a day, most days.

Which brings us to "The Silent Shot" (June 10, 1922), the first story of the series. Inspector Landers is stumped. There sprawls the body of District Attorney Robinson, dead of a .32 bullet to the temple. He lies in a soft chair in the smoking room of the exclusive Dearborn Club, his newspaper fallen beside his chair. The chair faces the window. The window overlooks Michigan Avenue, along which a parade just passed. The noise of the parade must have covered the sound of the shot, for none of the six prominent men in the room heard a thing. Or saw a thing. And the gun is missing.

Kincaid, the DA's bodyguard, is carrying an unfired .45, but you can't suspect so obvious a suspect. With great post-disaster efficiency,

Kincaid has detained the six prominent men until the police arrive. They arrive to be baffled.

It is an impossible crime

How glad Inspector Landers is when West arrives. "For the present, Mr. West, the investigation is in your hands." It is not the customary police routine, but these were unsettled times, and the story is only 8 1/2 pages long. Impossible crime or not, it must be solved in this issue. And it will be.

For, as West points out, "There is always something, you know, Mr. Inspector; the inexorable law of clews is the best ally that we have."

They look around the room, Miller spewing out a torrent of obvious observations. Then West questions all the suspects, which the police have forgotten to do. Obviously, the next step is to have them reenact their movements. By this time, West has observed a smudge of powder stains on the newspapers by the DA's chair. The police hadn't noticed this because the police have been shuffling their feet and clearing their throats.

The six prominent men move to their original positions. And one of them is carrying a cane--obviously a gun cane. You could tell from the smudge where the powder-stained tip touched the newspaper. And thus and so and....

"Through The Air" (July 29, 1922), another West triumph, succeeds because the police are blind, numb, and stupid. Particularly Detective Sergeant Burley, who is so ill-informed as to sneer at West and his new-fangled methods.

He, Burley, has already snared the murderer--rather, the murderess. She obviously shot her employer, Travis Whitson. Shot him right square in the head, right square in his electrical lab. This ungracious act followed a violent quarrel.

Heavens knows what she did with the gun. It has vanished away, as guns have a tendency to do in a Pinklin West case.

The girl, Norma Benson, claims she was leaving the lab when the shot came. And she didn't do it, didn't do it, didn't do it.

Thorne Miller: "A hunch tells me this girl didn't kill him."

Pinklin West: "Guessing! How many times have I warned you about that, Thorne?"

For once Miller is right. Norma didn't do it. As can be demonstrated by examining the dead man's ear, which is smeared with burnt powder. Then examining the telephone, which contains a pistol built into the receiver.

Burley never got around to examining the receiver, since this is a story in which the police must appear in the worst possible light, enabling Mr. West to glare and glitter all the more. But as soon as West saw that ear....

The shot was fired by a radio signal sent, as one might say, "Through The Air". Since the murderer had to know when Whitson had the receiver to his ear, the murderer was obviously the other man on the telephone.

As this deduction is made, the murderer (who has been eavesdropping on the investigation by radio), laughs wildly, confesses in a great voice, and shoots himself. Nicely confirming West's analysis.

"Too Clever" (August 21, 1922) concerns a doctor found dead in his garage. It is obviously death by accidental carbon monoxide poisoning. You can tell. The fresh snow around the garage is marred only by prints of the dead man's shoes going in, and his housekeeper's tracks to and from the garage. These tracks are paralleled by a line of holes in the snow, as if someone had jabbed a broomstick down every forty inches. But holes mean nothing. How could they?

So why does West suspect murder? He listens to the housekeeper; he listens blank-faced to the doctor's brother (who longed for the dead man's fiancee). No clues at all.

Now West inspects the doctor's room. Discovers the open window and the clue of the partially snow-covered window sill. Discovers the clue of the gas jet. Looks under the bed and discovers the clue of the dead dog.

No clue is shared with the reader. You might think that West would comment on the phenomena of the dog under the bed:

"Say, Thorne, you'd never guess what I just saw under the bed...."

Not West. He says not a word. Just dusts off his knees and blinks. Oh, he's close, West is.

All these clues are held back till the end of the story. Then out they blaze, confounding the reader and the murderer, whose identity (since it wasn't the housekeeper) is tolerably easy to guess.

Miller nearly has a spasm explaining how clever West is. How astute. A wonder man, don't you agree, dear reader?

Dear reader can hardly respond, since he is choking on the explanation of the holes in the snow. Seems that the murdering brother carried the doctor dead from his gas-filled bed-room across the snow to the garage. Then he recrossed the snow on a pogo stick. This device never appears in the story. However, it must have left those holes, and that's proof enough for a Chicago criminologist.

After this horrendous swindle on the reader, West returns to his apartment house. He is inventing things up there in his lab. He has invented a new way to transmit fingerprints by telegraph 'le is now working out a new system of criminal identification, ten ..es more effective than fingerprinting. Craig Kennedy would be proud to boil a beaker with him.

Before West invents himself out of job, a new case arrives. Wealthy young Hulbert Chalmers has mailed his fiancee, Patricia Thayer, a hand-written, special delivery suicide note. Too late she enlists West's help. When they reach Chalmers's apartment, they find him shot behind a locked door.

West promptly calls for Detective Sergeant Burley, that hard-nosed scoffer of "Through The Air".

> The veteran headquarters man had begun his association by scoffing at Pinklin West's methods of crime deduction, and had wound up by being both his admirer and warm personal friend.

Burley is not convinced that the Chalmers matter is a case for homicide.

> Burley: "The trouble with you, West, is that you always want to make a mystery out of every case you get on".

West must be wrong. The building attendant testifies that Chalmers gave him a special delivery letter to mail the previous evening. His story is confirmed by playwright Fleming Bruce, who was visiting Chalmers at the time. Bruce remarks that Chalmers was nervous and distracted and sad. Ready for suicide, maybe.

No soap. West deduces murder, reasoning from such clues as the special water-marked paper in Bruce's rooms, an opened and resealed

envelope, the serene handwriting of the suicide note, and significant cut marks along the notes' upper edge.
These clues are not provided the reader, who would only misunderstand them.
Your intuition is correct. Bruce did it. He loved Patricia and could not endure losing her to Chalmers. Pretending a sprained hand, he dictated a page of play script to Chalmers, who kindly wrote it down. Part of the dictation included a suicide note—and there you are.

"And Then A Game of Golf" (December 2, 1922) occupies a few brisk hours one rainy morning. Burley calls West, urgent, urgent, to investigate a bank robbery. Just happened. $50,000 gone. Teller shot down. The police are doing something else important, which is why Burley calls on a criminologist for help.

The dying teller has identified his killer as Roger Fenley, the confidential secretary to the bank president. Seems impossible. At the time, Fenley was in a taxi cab, far away, riding to an appointment with the president.

The taxi driver is unshakable; the alibi is not. West exposes a complicated meshwork of impersonation, substitution, conspiracy, embezzlement, and secret marriage. The detection requires only a few hours. After that, the criminals are marched away and the rain stops. Now Thorne Miller can get in a round of golf.

One final case appeared—"Deadly Safety", March 3, 1923. With that the endless silence fell, inexorable as the stroke of a cleaver. Although a few readers wrote, urging more stories, none seem to have been published. Pinklin West's history was complete.

All this happened sixty-odd years ago in the flaming youth of the detective story.

What was acceptable then, in 1922, in the more casual popular magazines, is stylistic criminality today. Our present literary convention requires fair play with clues, realistically motivated characters, touches of psychological insight, a musky dab of sex. Good things all. But not immutable. These are the conventions of our time, the style that shapes our writing and guides our reading.

If these conventions now seem permanent, so did the rather different conventions of the past. As will the much different conventions of future detective fiction. Our present beliefs about literary merit did not trouble Thorne Miller, writing sixty years ago. How cheerfully he concealed clues. How irrational his police and their procedures. How repetitive his devices and motives.

To the last, he worked in the convention of his time, blithely indifferent to the real relationship between policeman and private investigator in the world of 1922. He seemed unconcerned that Pinklin West was as colorless a figure as ever melted into the page. He followed uncritically the tradition of Sherlock Holmes and Craig Kennedy.

But even the brightest sun sets at last, the most adept imitator fades. Today Pinklin West is interesting mainly as an example of a minor magazine detective series at the opening of the Twenties.

That the series was so brief is suggestive. Perhaps those distant readers and editors were less easily charmed than we believe. Perhaps a series so flawed could sustain itself only briefly. Perhaps Miller, whoever he was, tired of Pinklin West. Perhaps.

Only the very confident venture to explain why a series ended. We only know that success isn't as easy as it looks. That West, like so many others, vanished after six stories, leaving behind a few questions inconvenient to answer, an ambiguous footnote to the history of the detective story.

The Dr. Davie Novels of V.C. Clinton-Baddeley

Earl F. Bargainnier

The life of Victor Vaughan Reynolds Geraint Clinton Clinton-Baddeley (1900-1970) was a multi-faceted one. After receiving his M.A. at Cambridge, he was at various times an editor of the **Encyclopedia Britannica**; an actor in both England and the United States; the author of a number of original plays, adaptations, operettas, pantomimes, and radio scripts; also author of a significant study in dramatic history, **The Burlesque Tradition in the English Theatre after 1660**; the owner-manager of Jupiter Records, specializing in recordings of poetry; and a well-known reader of poetry, especially that of William Butler Yeats. During the last four years of his life, he turned to detective fiction, writing five novels, all featuring the cases of Dr. R. V. Davie, an English professor at Cambridge University; **Deaths Bright Dart** (1967), **My Foe outstretch'd Beneath the Tree** (1968), **Only a Matter of Time** (1969), **No Case for the Police** (1970), and the posthumous **To Study a Long Silence** (1972), whose final two chapters were completed on the basis of Clinton-Baddeley's outline by his nephew Mark Goullet. One can only speculate as to why Clinton-Baddeley waited until he was sixty-seven to begin writing detective fiction, but one possible answer is given by Dr. Davie in the final novel: "I would like to write about the times I have lived in, but not about myself in those times" (90). The novels are filled with the times, places, and activities that Clinton-Baddeley experienced, as well as his enthusiasms and prejudices--admittedly at times to the detriment of the detection. If he is not Clinton-Baddeley's alter ego, Dr. Davie is at the least a clever device by which his creator could "write about the times I have lived in".

Five elements of the novels give them a distinctive quality and deserve some consideration. First, they are late examples of the classical school of detective fiction. A second and obvious element is the role of Dr. Davie. Another is the comic nature of the novels. Frequently related to that comic nature are the many digressions on whatever interests Dr. Davie and his creator. Lastly, there is an unfortunately obtrusive strain of misogyny running through the novels.

Long after repeated reports of the demise of classical detective fiction, Clinton-Baddeley's novels remain faithful to its conventions. From literary or punning titles to the map of St. Nicholas's College in **Death's Bright Dart**, from the absence of described violence to the minor role of the police, from the carefully planted clues and accompanying misdirection to the varied unrelated red herrings, the novels follow the traditions of the between-the-wars detective fiction genre. Three of the novels are based upon a time puzzle--how was the murder committed in the time available--and one has a perfect alibi plot, again standard forms earlier days. The settings are also conventional: a scientific conference at Cambridge, a London club and a woman's college, a music festival in southern England, a Devon village, and a dramatic school in northern London, each providing a closed circle of suspects. One of Clinton-Baddeley's strengths is his ability to spread suspicion throughout those closed circles; he ranks among the detective novelists in this ability. Over and over, the logical possibilities, whether of opportunity or motive or both, are many. As is the case with so many of his colleagues, his victims are not particularly likable or worse, an aid in producing so many suspects. Though the motives may be contemporary--revenge on a Nazi concentration camp doctor, industrial spying, or drug trafficking, the last present in two novels—or the perennial greed, they are developed in the classical manner. Discovery of these motives is complicated by other non-murderous crimes--blackmail, adulterous love affairs, fraudulent or stolen antiques--by suicide or an unrelated murder, and by lies, evasion, or pranks for any numbers of reasons by suspects and witnesses. These items by no means exhaust the classical features of the novels, but they are enough to demonstrate where the roots of Clinton-Baddeley's novels lie. Added evidence is Davie's normally reading three detective novels each week, his favorite author and fictional detective being Annabel Champion and her Miss Murchiston, tributes to Agatha Christie and Miss Marple.

Though having a definite personality, Dr. Davie can hardly be considered the eccentric detective so prevalent in the classical genre; rather he is a genial, elderly bachelor professor, who is an aesthete, a Romantic--at least in his fondness for Keats, president of his college--known both as St. Nicholas's and as Saint Anastasius and the Magnificent Virgin Edwina's--until his retirement, and vain as to his clothes, for vanity "makes the world a possible place to live in" (**Time,** 55). Little is presented of his earlier life, except that he grew up in Tidwell St. Peters, Devon, to which he returns in (**No Case for the Police**). When, as he frequently does, he goes to London, he stays either at the Chesterfield, his club, or at the Gainsborough Hotel; the difference between these two eighteenth-century establishments is minimal. He does have definite likes and dislikes. The first includes regular afternoon naps, window shopping, precision of language, and London. Of the last he is "a delighted observer of the London pageant" (**Silence, 67**), as his many walks and bus rides detail. He admires paperweights and collects glass-enclosed snowstorms (one of which gives him an important clue). He is a connoisseur of teas, at his college he keeps six varieties and mixes them according to taste and need for stimulation or rest. But without question, his greatest pleasures are the theatre and music, especially opera, which will be considered later. Foremost among the things he dislikes are most changes from earlier times, though not all, as will be seen. Other dislikes include the melodramatic, exercise, sandwiches, the sub-dividing of old houses, and the indiscriminate use of first names, which he considers produce the "ghastly insincerity of B.B.C. disc jockeys" (**Silence, 34**). He has always been bored by **Lady Chatterley's Lover** and is even more irritated by "a lot of old fuddy-duddies" swearing that it is "a work of genius" (**Dart, 166**). Neither the likes or dislikes are the eccentricities of a Wimsey or Poirot, but simply the preferences of an elderly man--and his author.

However, as a detective, Davie is definitely in the classical mode. He is a ratiocinative detective, who observes, asks questions, and thinks. His thoughts can rove "with peculiar agility" (**Case, 57**), and he works by theory, which he recognizes as such: "A professional investigator might have objected that there was too much guesswork in his theory. Well, what of it? He was not the police. he was only considering the evidence in order to satisfy himself. Never mind how he got there" (**Dart, 204**). This desire to satisfy himself, rather than some abstract sense of justice, is his motivation as detective. he can even call it "a mean and vain desire": "Do I want justice done? I do not. I only want to exercise my mind. To be right!" (**Silence, 113**). His ability to reason through a mass of complex and confusing facts allows him to be right; he usually knows the identity of the murderer quite early, but refuse to reveal him or her for lack of evidence—another classical convention. he notes but is not overly interested in physical evidence. His favorite clues are those of human behavior upon which his mind can weave possible scenarios. His basic philosophy of detection is "Clues come to one by luck or diligence. Speculation belongs to the mind" (**Case, 207**).

Of course, there must be evidence to support the theories, and he finds it. he is aided by his age and geniality which cause people to confess to him about their lives as they would not to others, especially the police. His sleuthing, or more precisely, snooping, for evidence is not limited to the strictly legal. In each of the five novels he trespasses in one way or another to obtain information. He may gain entrance under false pretenses, may enter unobserved, or even break a window and crawl through to "steal" evidence that he must have to prove his theory. That such activity is illegal is of little concern to him, and that it is dangerous, particularly for a man of his age, is even less so: "He feared violence. But he did not fear danger. He rather enjoyed a calculated risk" (**Dart, 161**). All in all, though more active, Davie as detective is much like a male Miss Marple, whose adventures disguised as Miss Murchiston's he so admires.

Much of the novel's comic nature is the result of Davie's personality, but other elements contribute. There are incongruous bits, such as the questioning of how to say thanks to a Mr. Thankful or to write a letter to a Mr. Dear (Dear Dear:), or a brochure advertising a Russian army choir singing "Gaily the Friendly Tanks Roll By", "Hark to the Kremlin Bells", and other "similar favourites" **Silence, 17**. Also present in four of the novels are anthropomorphic cats. Davie talks to Reginald (**Foe**), Tommy (**Time**), Blanche (**Case**), and an unnamed black-and-white cat (**Silence**) as if they were human, and they all respond warmly to him, especially Reginald, whose owner describes him as "gay—in the modish sense of the word". None, however, have a part in the mysteries of the novels. The same is true of subsidiary characters, who are comic but irrelevant. Miss Mercer of Reception at the Gainsborough; Miss Christabelle Mittens, cashier of the Chesterfield; Mr. Jump and Mrs. Pilsworthy, porter and maid of St. Nicholas's are amusing and sometimes surprising versions of the **hoi polloi**. Similarly comic, if on a higher social level, are members of the Chesterfield, such as the rather pompous George Cantaloupe, the inveterate talker Conway Gordon, and the eccentric grouch Frederick Dyke. His fellow opera and concert-goers, including Lady Mildred Meade-Fuller, who knows everyone, and the monstrous Mrs. Maud Mapleton-Morley and her put-upon niece Miss Bangles, also provide comic interludes. The fatuous undergraduates, pseudo-radical Baggs and pseudo-sophisticated Mostyn-Humphries, and the no-nonsense principal of a woman's college, Miss Eggar, and her cats are still other examples of Clinton-Baddeley's comic characterization. Among numerous others, these comic characters form the background, the atmosphere, of the novels. Though unnecessary for the investigative plot—not one of the above is a witness or suspect—they contribute significantly to the Sheridanesque tone of the novels.

Just as these characters are irrelevant to the action, so are most of Davie's observations on matters non-detectival, usually nostalgic or theatrical-musical. One technique that any detective novelist must master is the protracting of mystery without the protraction being obvious; Clinton-Baddeley apparently did not care whether it was obvious or not. One basic method was the nostalgic reminiscences of Davie. **No Case for the Police** is as much a nostalgic novel of an old man's remembering his youth as it is a detective novel (the murder is also in the past) and is the least satisfying of the five as the latter. Similar digressions occur in the other novels, triggered by sights on Davie's walks or bus rides through the streets of London of by some object which reminds him of earlier times and the way life once was. it is to be expected that an observant, sensitive, elderly gentleman would notice change and recall the past with nostalgia, and Clinton-Baddeley uses this expectation to make comments, often quite witty, on changes in England during this century.

Equalling the number of reminiscent digressions are those on matters theatrical and musical. Comic presentations of theatre and opera audiences, their conversations and their pretensions; satire of music critics;,good-natured mockery of the teaching of acting; discussion of plays and players, revivals of long-forgotten works, the inadequacy of sheer fakery of some performers--all appear. Davie attends a rock concert by Jack Wraith and the Seven Deadly Sins, which he summarizes as "a dress rehearsal for the Last Trump" (**Dart, 192**), but he enjoys a student production of **As You Like It**, which transforms Shakespeare's characters into gangsters and hippies. In **Only a Matter of Time** he attends a concert of "Jazz and Poetry", and over three pages are devoted to a satiric sendup of the **avant-garde**. One of the performers is Persephone Popondopoulos, who first sings jazz versions of Elizabeth Barrett Browning and then:

> She ended the first part of the program with a lyric by a contemporary poet, singing against a recording of herself singing against a recording of herself singing against a recording of herself, thereby creating a work in four parts for one voice. At one point Miss Popondopoulos sang into the bell of a trumpet. At another she placed her head inside the grand piano. She also sang roguishly through the strings of the harp. (157)

Oddly enough, Davie is "enchanted" by her performance.

The only novel in which there is any integration of the theatrical matter and the mystery is **To Study a long Silence**, which consequently is the best structured of the novels. The murder occurs at a **commedia dell' arte** performance given by the students of the Winston (Churchill?) School of Acting, thus providing for comment on this traditional form of pantomime. Davie is presented as an expert on it, as Clinton-Baddeley certainly was, and its use by Richard Strauss in **Ariade auf Naxos** explains the repeated references in the novels to that being Davie's favorite opera.

One other topic for digression is food. The proper way to prepare zabaglione, risotto, halibut, and avocado soup, the delectability of a New Zealand Pavlova, and the full recipe for a proper **creme de brulee** are all included. One can only wonder, with such tastes, if Clinton-Baddeley had the waistline that Davie admits to being "certainly 37." The point is that Clinton-Baddeley did not hesitate to add his own enthusiasms, most of which are delightful, to his novels, and their absence would remove much of the novels' fun.

The only problematic aspect of the novels is the misogynistic strain present. davie likes old or eccentric ladies; younger women are scorned unless they are useful by being brisk and efficient. He finds fault with "lunatic" women who feed pigeons, those who wear pants or show their "horrible knees" in short skirts, and those who wear lilac lipstick, which he says makes them "look like somebody recently raised from the dead" (**Dart, 87**). A woman appears in **My Foe Outstretch'd Beneath the Tree** with no other function than to permit Davie to fulminate against her appearance:

> Davie had many pet dislikes: the plucked eyebrow, the painted cupid's bow which fails to conceal the thin cruel lip of a rapacious strumpet, the dark parting which betrays the truth about a head of golden hair. That especially gave him the willies. This lady, undoubtedly handsome, notably well-dressed, exhibited all the marks of Jezebel. She also wore long adhesive talons of obscenely varnished ebony. (17)

All the novels contain such bitterly satirical portraits of women, often of women who would normally be considered attractive, but in none of the others is there as much as in **Only a Matter of Time**. It includes Mrs. Copplestone, a "sweetly" domineering mother; Mrs. Rowan, a weak and tasteless wife; Mrs. Bazeley, a repulsive and greedy antique dealer; and "Madame Jeanne, Hair styles, nee Shirley Muffin", about whom is the following unnecessarily snide passage:

> A nice ordinary young woman in her late twenties—though she looked older because she thought well to bleach one of her dark locks a silver grey. Her lady customers considered this smart, and so did Shirley, but the more simple men of King's Lacy thought it was hard luck that a nice girl like Shirley should go grey so prematurely. They did not know that women make up not to attract men but to stun other women. Girls think they can best defeat the men with their hidden weapons. And they are right: only a very pure young man falls for a woman's face. (111)

This misogyny is paralleled by Davie's pleasure in the company of young men and "leering" remarks about young men's bodies. There is nothing patently homosexual in the attitude expressed, but an undercurrent that makes this reader wish either for more openness or its elimination. In **No Case for the Police** and **To Study a Long Silence**, Davie is aided by attractive young men, neither of whom has a girl friend, while in **My Foe Outstretch'd Beneath the Tree** the homosexual murder of young actor Andrew Wynne, hardly related to the central plot, distresses Davie greatly. His reminiscences of his early life in **No Case for the Police** center on his friendship with Robert Cassilis and his disappointment when he married "a dragon" and Davie realized that "three was very poor company indeed", but "everybody" was "secretly relieved when she walked off the end of a jetty one night" (15). Needless to say, like his creator, Davie has never married. After a long digression on the meaning of **camp,** he says, "The man who marries abandons liberty. He doesn't always enjoy the experience--doesn't often, I believe, I could say. I'm sure I wouldn't" (**Foe, 111.** He then adds of Reginald, his hostess' anti-female cat, "He is comfort-loving but also man-loving" (112).

Davie can be amused by an overheard conversation of a group of "airy gentlemen" while on vacation, but when he sees one of them later on the beach "wearing nothing but a light blue triangle" and looking like a "figure of mahogany", he says to his companion, "my attention was diverted by the pursuit of beauty" (**Dart, 208-9**). In **Only a Matter of Time** there are remarks on the suggestive costumes worn by two young men as Oberon and Puck, and in **To Study a Long Silence** other comments on codpieces and the hilarious results of a young actor wearing tights without a codpiece--"though truly, in some respects, the episode had enhanced his reputation" (44). In the same novel Davie is invited backstage to the men's dressing room, where he is aware of a young man "naked, hairy, sexy, and blushing" (111). A final example concerns the visit of Martin Searle, the young actor who aids davie, to the Chesterfield immediately after the hope is expressed that women will return to ankle-length dresses:

> Martin Searle was dressed most becomingly. Vain, as Davie was vain, he enjoyed his clothes and spent too much on them. His trousers were wide at the ends, close at the knees, and in the more northerly parts fitted him like a skin. He wore a white shirt with a sapphire blue tie and a deep blue velvet jacket. ...Sitting down he looked like someone in a Jane Austen novel. Standing up he looked like the present. That was the trousers. ...at least three members of the club took a long look at Martin looking at the ticker tape. It was not often that the Chesterfield saw anything as ornamentally suitable within its eighteenth century walls. (135-36, 138)

Whether conscious or unconscious—and I doubt the latter—the novels do have this strain of denigration of women and praise of male physicality. It is present again and again and cannot be denied.

On the other hand, this strain is apparent only upon reading all of the novels in sequence and more than once, whereas the classical conventions, the genial role of Dr. Davie, the comedy and the digressions are immediately evident. Supporting, or perhaps overarching, all of these elements is Clinton-Baddeley's style. Witty, urbane, sophisticated, ironic, satiric: any of these could be used to describe it. it is the style of high comedy--farce plays no part--and probably the best adjective is **theatrical.** If, as I believe, Clinton-Baddeley wrote these novels essentially to comment through Davie upon his likes and dislikes, what could be more appropriate for a man of the theatre to turn to classical detective fiction which has so often been compared to the comedy of manners. Clinton-Baddeley's long association with stage comedy as actor and author made the choice an obvious one. The novels succeed as comedy, as nostalgia, and as detective novels (four of the five are available in paperback in the United States). **[And the fifth will be soon]** One can only wish that Clinton-Baddeley had decide earlier "to write about the times I have lived in" and to use the detective novel for his structure. His last novel has the prophetic title from Webster's **The White Devil** of **To Study a Long Silence,** silence being death. He did not finish the novel, and when it is said of Dr. Davie in the last line that "Secretly, peacefully he crossed the frontiers of sleep" (192), the effect is of both detective and author having ended their existence and entered that inescapable long silence, but leaving behind five novels to give pleasure, whatever their faults, to others still awaiting it.

Can We Reach Agreement?

J.R. Christopher

As a notice "About the Author" announces at the end of Emma Lathen's **Green Grow the Dollars** (New York: Simon and Schuster, 1982), Lathen "is the nom de plume shared by Mary Jane Latsis, an economist, and Martha Henissart, a lawyer." I do not know how aware economists are of the English language, but lawyers are usually very precise in their usage. And certainly the two women who write as Emma Lathen have always seemed to me very exact stylists.

All of this is in preparation for a sentence which occurs in Chapter 22 of **Green Grow the Dollars**. The speaker is Mary Larrabee of North Dakota, who in the novel has developed an improved sweet pea and who suddenly had become wealthy through home-gardening endorsements. She is speaking of a secretary at an agricultural laboratory who had taken some money to send information about an improved tomato to a person at another laboratory, and who had been killed after she went to pieces emotionally upon learning what the legal and financial results were. Mrs. Larrabee says, "After all, she'd trusted **somebody** to advise her and **they'd** taken advantage of her" (emphasis added, p. 180). This is faulty agreement in number: **somebody** is singular, **they** is plural.

What would cause Emma Lathen to produce this simple grammatical mistake? I can think of four possibilities. First, it might be an attempt to characterize Mary Larrabee: she is speaking an uneducated English. This is possible; certainly she is depicted as a very shrewd but not erudite person. All I can say against it is that this is the only faulty agreement I noticed in her language. She is often colloquial, but she does not seem given to linguistic errors.

Second, it might be an error on the part of Emma Lathen. The authors simply did not catch the shift in number. Again it is possible, but it does not seem likely. Besides the authors, it would also have had to get by their editor at Simon and Schuster. Of course, editors, these days, are rather uncertain in their abilities, but still.... At any rate, this would necessitate at least three people--and probably a proofreader and maybe others in addition--missing the error.

Third, it might be a feminist statement. Feminists are bothered by the traditional "singular noun ... he" structure, arguing that it builds a masculine bias into the language (and they are surely right). Grammatically, Larrabee could have said, ". . . she'd trusted **somebody** to advise her and **he or she** had taken advantage of her"; but most of us do not colloquially use the "he or she" structure. On the other hand, Larrabee does not seem to be a liberated woman in matters beyond finances. She might be likely to use the universal masculine as she had been taught to do in school. In this reading, the authors could not stand the single masculine pronoun and so used a deliberate shift in

number, for which, indeed, some feminists have argued.
Fourth, it might be a deliberate detective-novel ploy. Mary Larrabee, given her background, probably would have used **he**, but Emma Lathen did not want such a clear-cut reference to a single masculine malefactor--because that was the way the novel was going to turn out. Thus, she used a vaguer, although grammatically incorrect, **they**, in order to suggest the whole group at the trival laboratory, or the whole group at the seed company which sponsored the rival laboratory's work, generally and indistinctly. Again, this assumes that the authors deliberately distorted Larrabee's likely language for their own purposes.

Which one of these is true? Or is there a possibility I have not considered? I doubt that the cause will ever be determined; but nevertheless a solecism, which I find regretful in Emma lathen's novel, exists.

GRISE NOTES (continued from page 46): print. After years of carping criticisms from young Stilwell, both in these pages and--even more obnoxiously--in personal communications, I cannot resist observing that when I hurriedly ran the copy for this issue through my spelling checker I found one hundred and fifteen spelling errors (not counting repeat misspellings of the same words), and, because of my haste, there are probably others that I missed. That's two and a half spelling errors per page. Obviously, we've got to get our new editor fitted out with a functioning speller right away.

A couple of words of apology regarding the last two issues of 1983. One regards the faint quality of the print. The characters on the printwheel I have used ever since TMF went on computer are rather thin to start with, and, as a result of the horrible conditions under which I had to do the darkroom work on 7:5 and 7:6--exposing the negatives at the shop and developing them in the bathroom at home, then burning and developing the plates in my kitchen--I was unaware that I had used too long an exposure time until all the work was done. Even had I been willing to throw away hundreds of dollars worth of materials--and I don't suppose I have to tell you that doing so would have gone completely against my nature--I didn't have the time to do it over again. So the last two issues were real squinters. This time out I should be able to do all of the work at one place, so those problems should not repeat themselves. And, I have finally managed to find a bolder typeface for my printer, which should result in far more legible copy this time around.

No doubt you also noticed another screw up regarding 7:5 and 7:6. I printed out the camera-ready copy for both issues at the same time, and 7:5 was supposed to run to a full fifty pages, while 7:6, because of the postal regulation that requires the publication of a statement of ownership once a year, was to run to forty-nine pages, with said statement appearing on the back cover. Well, when I was taping the pages together preparatory to photographing them, I stupidly taped page fifty on 7:6 and the statement of ownership on 7:5. Which is why Jane Bakerman's review of Margaret Yorke's **Devil's Work** is cut off in mid-sentence on page forty-nine of 7:5 and resumes just as abruptly on page fifty of 7:6.

Well, enough of this blather. All things considered, I think Steve has done a fine job on his first issue, and I'm sure we'll get the minor glitches ironed out after another issue or two.

In personal letters which I have not had time to answer, several of you have asked about the progress of my legal education, so I'll take this easy way of answering you all at once. (Continued on page 22)

IT'S ABOUT CRIME by Marvin Lachman

NOTES ON RECENT READING

In Jon Breen's first novel the horse racing background provides a nice bonus to a fast-paced mystery that can stand on it's own. Another extra is the way Breen works "in jokes" about the mystery genre to his own book. What else could one expect from the best parodist of the field, also an "Edgar" winner for his critical work, **What About Murder?** I especially enjoyed Breen's beer-drinking horse, "Pfui" and the including of Silver Blaze with Man O' War, Citation, and the other great horses of all time.

Listen to the Click grabs the reader's attention quickly with the murder of a leading jockey who is seated astride the statue of a famous horse. The cast of suspects is large, but Breen usually succeeds in individualizing each for the reader, even those who make only token appearances. Though he could (and probably eventually will) write an old-fashioned mystery with lots of clues and timetable alibis, he has not done so here; though this **is** a detective story. In fact, there are probably too many detectives, no fewer than five, though Jerry Brogan, race track announcer, is responsible for the ultimate solution. The plotting here is not especially complex and the key clue, for a reader wanting to play detective, is a relatively easy one to spot. It must be, I spotted it. Where **Listen for the Click** shines is in it's pace, dialogue and authentic characters. It was published by Walker at $12.95.

Metzger's Dog (Scribner's $14.95) is about the dog that was tamed by the cat in the novel that Thomas Perry built. Also residing in this madhouse are three Vietnam Vets who have their own home-made cannon and pull off big capers. By chance they get involved with the CIA whom they blackmail for about $600,000. Somehow, the city of Los Angeles is held hostage. It's wild, crazy, and I didn't believe a word of it. I had fun.

Just out in paperback is Perry's first mystery, **The Butcher's Boy**(Charter $2.95), winner of the "Edgar" as Best First Novel of 1982. Again, the ingredients are unlikely: Mafia hit men, Justice Department agents, and a U.S. Senator. With just a little willing suspension of disbelief, one will find that it all works and that this is an oddly plausible, thoroughly exciting book.

A fascinating article in **Smithsonian** in 1982 was an excerpt from Ben Weider and David Hapgood's book, **The Murder of Napoleon**, reprinted by Berkley at $3.50. The authors prove that sometimes truth is stranger (and even more interesting) than fiction as they detail the efforts of a Swedish investigator to prove that Napoleon did not die of stomach cancer as generally supposed. He apparently was the victim of arsenic poisoning. Readers who enjoyed **The Daughter of Time** are only a small percent of the people who should enjoy this exercise in medical detection. Incidentally, this well-illustrated book was a selection of the both the Book-of-the-Month Club and the History Book Club.

Still Available from Pocket Books is another fine Dick Francis thriller, **Risk** (1977), in which the author, as usual, "hooks" the reader on page one. By the end of the first chapter you probably couldn't stop reading if your life depended on it, that's how well Francis involves us in the danger to his hero, whose life **does** depend on it. This time the hero is an accountant with many horse owners and jockeys as clients. He is also an amateur steeplechase rider good enough to win the Gold Cup. As he says of his love of riding, "Addiction wasn't only a matter of needles in the arm." The same could be said of mystery reading and collecting. As is usual in Dick Francis books, **Risk** contains stoical heroism, unspeakable villainy, and many surprises. There is also a discreet, but surprisingly erotic, handling of sex which could serve as an object lesson to unsubtle authors in this overly-explicit age.

Not just to be read in October is another in Avon's excellent series of topical short story collections edited by Asimov, Greenberg, and Waugh. This one, **The 13 Horrors of Halloween** ($2.95), includes that marvelous Ellery Queen story, "The Adventure of the Dead Cat" and a tale with a genuinely chilling ending, Ray Bradbury's "The October Game".

If I use the term "Soap Opera" in the pejorative sense, it is because I have never been a fan of that type of drama. As a child, I occasionally tuned in to them on radio if I was home sick from school. I seldom managed to make it through an entire show, except for **Perry Mason** which, while not strictly a "soap", did come on at the same time, If anything my tolerance for them on television is less, but now I get to ignore them both in the afternoon and in the evening where they have risen from the ashes like the fabled Dallas bird.

E.X. Ferrars' **Depart this Life** (1958) is a "Soap Opera" of a mystery. It is basically about domestic quarrels and problems, with occasional interludes of mystery. There is seemingly endless dialogue, much of it repeated for what appears to be padding. For example:

"Of course it isn't true", Hilda said.
After a moment Katherine drew away from her.
"How do you know it isn't?" she asked.
"Shouldn't I have known of it, if it were?" Hilda said.
"And you didn't?"

or

"But my own child, Katherine, How am I to deal with her?"
"Do you mean...?" She paused uneasily. "You don't mean, do you, that you're thinking of interfering with this marriage?" she said.
"Is that what I said?" he asked.
"I'm not sure...then that is what you meant."

When I wrote the article on Ferrars for the **Encyclopedia of Mystery and Detection**, I felt a bit guilty afterward because I had quoted Barzun and Taylor who said: "Her people and plots are so standard." Perhaps, I hadn't read enough of her work, and that is why I agreed with them. If **Depart this Life** is an example, I may actually have read too much.

John D. MacDonald is the last of the great mystery writers to have gotten his start in the pulps. He wrote hundreds of stories during the last few years pulps were published, and Harper and Row wisely collected 13 of them in **The Good Old Stuff** at $14.95 (reprinted by Fawcett in paper at $3.50). The early JDM may not have been quite as smooth a writer as the current JDM, but he was awfully good for a newcomer. Both MacDonalds are excellent story-tellers.

In his foreword, MacDonald refers to Park Falkner, who appears in two of the stories, as a "precursor" of McGee, but I see little similarity. If McGee had enough money, he probably would completely give up his "salvage" work and spend the rest of his life on "vacation". Falkner is wealthy enough to do that, but he is bored and so occupies himself as "a dilettante of crime". He invites house guests with hidden pasts to his Florida estate. seeking to arouse conflicts and, incidentally, solve crimes. His physical appearance also is different from McGee since, though he is also tall, he is very slim and completely hairless due to a tropical disease. The biggest Falkner-McGee similarity is in quality. "From Some Hidden Grave", though much shorter, is as good as some of the McGee novels.

MacDonald has updated some of the topical references, but otherwise the stories are unchanged. At risk of being what he would call a "purist", I wish he hadn't. For example, he felt that modern readers would not know Primo Canera and substituted Superman instead. It is not, in any way, crucial to enjoying the stories, but i wish he assumed the 1983 reader who didn't recognize Carnera (who was very unlike Superman) would be interested in looking him up. This is how, as a bonus, when we are reading strictly for pleasure, information can be passed from one generation to the next.

The Good Old Stuff contains another of what has become Francis M. Nevins' specialities: the insightful introduction which is combined with a succinct biography of the author. It makes **The Good Old Stuff** even better.

There is a surprising amount in McGraw-Hill's **Encyclopedia of Frontier and Western Fiction** ($29.95), edited by Jon Tuska and Vicki Piekarski, that should be of interest to mystery fans. Firstly, murder and other crimes are an important part of both genres. Secondly, many writers, included in this encyclopedia have written mysteries. To name a few--Max Brand, Brian Garfield, Elmore Leonard, W.T. Ballard, and Tony Hillerman. In one of the few errors in this reference work, whoever wrote the article on Hillerman calls **The Fly on the Wall** a western. Not so. I'll bet that the article was not written by Robert E. Briney who is a contributing editor to this book, as he was to **Encyclopedia of Mystery and Detection**. Talk about your literary hat tricks! Is there anyone as knowledgeable in three separate genres, Mystery, Western, and SF as is Briney?

This is a fine and useful reference work though it has two weaknesses, considering its price. Its illustrations lack both quantity and variety. They are limited primarily to photos of the more famous writers. Also, there is a condescending attitude to some of the genre writers whose work is consistently described as "formulary". I question the editors' devoting as much space as is given to mainstream writers such as Willa Cather, Mark Twain, John Steinbeck, et al. Their presence justifies the first adjective in the title, but their biographies can be found in almost any standard reference work on authors. I wish this encyclopedia had included writers like E.E. Halleran, Frank O'Rourke, and Jack Ehrlich instead.

Academy of Chicago, 425 N. Michigan Ave, Chicago, IL 60611, is quietly becoming one of the most interesting publishers of quality mysteries, both on their own and with the International Polygonics (IP) line. Academy has helped save the work of Leo Bruce from being forgotten, publishing many of the books in his two series regarding Sergeant Beef and Carolus Deene. They also distribute a marvelous series of paperback British true crime books, e.g. **Jack the Ripper: The Final Solution** by Stephen Knight ($5.95); **The Murderer's Who's Who: 150 Years of Notorious Murder Cases** by Gaute and Odell ($6.95); **Bernard Spilsbury: Famous Murder Cases of the Great Pathologist** by Douglas. G. Browne and Tom Tullett ($5.95).

International Polygonics has gathered the last mystery writing Dashiell Hammett did, the X-9 comic strips, into a trade paperback at $9.95. Though the book's major appeal is due to our love of nostalgia, many of the strips can stand on their own due to the detective elements Hammett inserted, like a locked room shooting and a cryptogram. Of course, the detection is primitive, and the writing generally of comic book caliber. After all, this was a comic strip.

International Polygonics has also been reprinting the work of Margaret Millar, that great writer, who with her late husband, Ross Macdonald (Kenneth Millar), made up the most talented household in the genre. Published so far are **A Stranger in My Grave** (1960) and **How Like an Angel** (1962), both with brief but interesting Millar introductions describing how the books were written. As novels, they tell a great deal about life in California, but they never forget that they're mysteries and the elements of puzzle and suspense are always present. What sets them really apart is that the characters are so multi-dimensioned and believable. Each book is $5.00, but don't be put off by the price of these or any of the other books distributed by Academy Chicago. These are attractive, well-made paperbacks which look as if they will last forever. With the quality of books like the Millars, they deserve to.

1983 was another banner year for **Ellery Queen's Mystery Magazine**, with an average quality of story that is consistently high. I found the following, in order, to be the best, but once again, many very good stories had to be eliminated.

1. James Powell-"The Scarlet Totem"
2. Clark Howard-"Wild Things"
3. Ruth Rendell-"Loopy"
4. Barbara Callahan-"Have You Seen This Women"
5. Edward D. Hoch-"Suddenly in September"
6. Howard-"Puerto Rico Blues"
7. Maralyn Horsdal-"An Educated Taste"
8. Howard-"New Orleans Getaway"
9. Howard-"Custer's Ghost"
10. Patricia Moyes-"The Faithful Cat"

Though Powell's hilarious story about Maynard Bullock of the Canadian Mounties was the single most enjoyable story of the year, the big story of 1983 in EQMM was the emergence of Clark Howard as the outstanding mystery short story writer around today. He wrote no fewer than four of the top ten short stories of the year, an impressive achievement. The best first story, by Maralyn Horsdal, made such effective use of food and wine that it left me not only hungry for a good dinner but for more stories by this gifted new writer.

Several trends regarding EQMM should be noted. Firstly, the content has kept up with the times. There is a willingness now to publish crime stories involving human sexuality and also to include relatively strong language occasionally. The key is that there is neither sex nor scatology for its own sake.. When used, they are always essential to the story.

Secondly, the covers continue to be more imaginative than they once were. For the first twenty years its life, EQMM's covers were excellent, including the drawings of such artists as George Salter, Ed Emsh, and Milton Glaser. There were also some imaginatively, well-staged photographs. Beginning in the mid 1950's there was a gradual change. Some readers, mostly female subscribers, complained about an excess of gore and the undraped female form, though I feel they had over reacted in both regards. EQMM accommodated them by doing a separate, blander cover for mailing. (These are now collector's items). By 1961, pictorial covers became the exception, and the cover of almost every issue looked like its predecessor and its successor. From correspondence with Fred Dannay in 1961, I gathered that the reasons were economic, involving the availability of art work at a price EQMM felt it could afford. Things changed in the late 1970's, and EQMM readers were given, successively, art work, portraits of the great detectives, photographs of mystery writers, and, now, photographs depicting crimes.

As one who originally bought EQMM when it was 25 cents, I am well aware that it's newstand price is now $1.75 (much less to mail subscribers). It is still a bargain, with about 150 pages of short stories, reviews, and interviews each issue. I have every issue of EQMM and am looking forward to issue #500, which, if my calculations are correct, should be the January 1985 number.

The Man Who Heard too Much by Stockton Woods (a pseudonym of Richard Forrest) from Fawcett Gold Medal at $2.50, almost went into my discard pile after I had read only a few pages and discovered it was about the usual venal U.S. Senator hatching the usual dastardly plot. Then, I was hooked when it turned out that only a retarded young man could spoil this plot, and the Senator was sending a team of killers after him. Believable? Barely. Readable and exciting? Very definitely.

In biographical and autobiographical material, Georges Simenon has said he made love to 10,000 women! He also complained a great deal about his family and the terrible pressures of writing. They cause him to require sex after he has finished one of his novels, typically in only seven to ten days. Except for working on his autobiography, Simenon has done no knew writing in over a decade. Thus, his mystery career appears to have ended with both a bang and a whimper. **The Lodger**, recently published by Harcourt at $12.95, is a non-Maigret novel dating from 1934, and it is a good example of why I prefer his work about the inspector.

Set in Simenon's Belgium, **The Lodger** is about people who can never come alive and are so obnoxious, one does not want to know them--alive or dead. The hero (Hah!) kills during a train robbery and hides at the boarding house run by the parents of his girl friend, the heroine (hah!). As the police close in, the titular character becomes increasingly agoraphobic, staying in a small room most of the time. The reader becomes increasingly claustrophobic. Novels like **The Lodger** are usually called Simenon's psychological thrillers, but I have found much more thrilling and readable material in psychological text books.

NOTES ON RECENT VIEWING

Where else but on commercial television would a series pilot called **Murder Ink**, about a book store of that name, be filmed at The

Mysterious Bookshop? The failed pilot was aired on CBS in early September 1983, and I, for one, am not too disappointed, based on what I saw, that we won't have a series. The plot to **Murder Ink** may have been far-fetched, but the acting was mediocre. Tovah Feldshuh was no more than adequate as Laura Ireland, owner of a bookstore specializing in mysteries, who gets to solve a murder because her husband is a police sergeant. The least problem with **Murder Ink** was a reference to an imaginary 1942 Mickey Spillane book, **The Frozen Dagger**, by a supposed mystery expert. It was said so quickly that even devout mystery fans watching may have missed it. They certainly missed the closing credits which went by so fast as to be unwatchable.

DEATH OF A MYSTERY WRITER

This time, in two cases, mystery deaths were a bit more sensational than usual.
1. **Norah Lofts** on September 10, 1983 at age 79 in Bury St. Edmunds, England. Better known for her historical novels, she wrote mysteries as Peter Curtis **The Devil's Own**-1960 and under her own name **Checkmate**-1975. A posthumous collection of her short stories is due from Doubleday in February 1984. I hope it will include her very good mystery short, "The Man on The Telephone" (1970).
2. **Beverly Nichols** on September 15, 1983 at age 85 in Kingston-on-Thames near London. An Oxford graduate, Mr Nichols was a gossip columnist and playwright as well as the author of fifty books, including five detective stories (1954-1960) about a series character, Horatio Green.
In his 1972 autobiography, **Father Figure**, Nichols admitted to having tried to kill his alcoholic father on three different occasions. At age 15 he slipped crushed aspirin into his father's soup. Next, he ran a heavy roller over him as he napped on the lawn. The third time he administered a heavy dose of sleeping pills and left his father in the snow. Each time Nichol's father survived, and he, too, died at age 85, of natural causes.
3. **Muriel Davidson** on September 26, 1983 at age 59 in Los Angeles' fashionable Benedict Canyon. Davidson wrote three mystery novels as well as episodes for the **Baretta** television series. At the time of her death, she was Vice-president of film and television development for Jay Bernstein Productions.
Davidson was shot to death. A 51 year old radar expert in the aerospace industry, whom she had counseled in an alcoholic rehabilitation program as a volunteer, was arrested and charged with her murder.
4. **Robert C. Dennis** on September 14, 1983 at age 67 in Hollywood, California. Born in Ontario, Canada, Dennis was best known for his television scripts, doing more than 500 for such mystery shows as **Perry Mason, Alfred Hitchcock Presents, Charlie's Angels, Dragnet, Cannon, and Barnaby Jones**. He also created **Passport to Danger** which starred Cesar Romero. He wrote two mystery novels which were published by Bobbs-Merrill, **The Sweat of Fear** (1973) and **Conversation with a Corpse**(1974).
5. **Zenith Jones Brown** on August 25, 1983 at age 84 in Baltimore. Mrs. Brown wrote more than sixty mysteries, between the years 1928 and 1962, under the pseudonyms Leslie Ford and David Frome. Her first Frome books were written while she was in England accompanying her husband, Professor Ford K. Brown, who was in London on a Guggenheim scholarship. As Frome she wrote 11 novels and at least one short story about timid Evan Pinkerton and his friend, Inspector Bull of Scotland

Yard.

Her Ford stories were even better known, especially the fifteen regarding an attractive widow, Grace Latham, and her friend, Colonel Primrose, formerly of Army Intelligence. They were enormously popular and were often serialized in **The Saturday Evening Post** before book publication.

6. **W. Todhunter Ballard** on December 27, 1980 at age 74 in Mount Dora, Florida. Ballard's death three years ago passed unnoticed in any newspapers I saw. I became aware of it through the article on him in **The Encyclopedia of Frontier and Western Fiction** and then almost simultaneously, when John Apostolou sent me a eulogy for Ballard, written for **The Roundup**, a Western Writers publication, by William R. Cox.

Ballard was an extremely popular writer in the pulps, especially **Black Mask**, with his series about Bill Lennox, movie trouble shooter. He wrote four books about Lennox, one of which was published as by John Shepherd. He also wrote mysteries under the pseudonyms P.D. Ballard, Neil MacNeil, and, with Norbert Davis, Harrison Hunt. Most of the latter part of Ballard's career was as a western writer, and he achieved great popularity in that genre as well. His hardcover Western, **Gold in California**, won the Western Writers of America "Spur" award in 1965.

GRISE NOTES (continued from page 15): So far, I have not managed to flunk out. Starting next week, I will be attending school four nights a week, instead of three, for a weekly commute of more than 600 miles, so if you are kind enough to write to me, please don't be offended if it's six or eight months before I get around to replying. The regular night-school program runs a full four years, but when you land on the wrong side of forty time suddenly becomes much more valuable, so I have successfully petitioned for permission to graduate in three years instead. Since the first year has just ended, that means that I've got to squeeze three years of school into two.... I'm thinking about hiring someone to eat my meals for me.

Ooops! I almost forgot. Here's a bit of good news for TMFers, both as mystery readers and (come on, admit it) as would-be mystery writers. Perseverance Press (P.O. Box 384, Menlo Park, CA 94025) is a new publishing house devoted to publishing mysteries in a 6" x 9" trade paperback format. PP has one mystery in print so far--Meredith Phillips' **Death Spiral**, about murder at the Winter Olympics--and it is a handsome book in the Dover tradition. (I haven't had time to read it yet--where would I find time?--but my clerk read it last week and pronounced it a fine book.) The price is $6.95 at your mystery bookstore, or $8.00 postpaid from the above address.

Here's what PP is after: "Perseverance Press is actively soliciting mystery manuscripts of the old-fashioned sort, e.g. who dunits, puzzlers, 'village cozies,' and others without excessive gore. Sex must not be exploitive or violent. Models for prospective authors include Agatha Christie, Josephine Tey, Dorothy L. Sayers, Antonia Fraser, Amanda Cross, Lucille Kallen, Margaret Millar, P.D. James, Simon Brett, Sheila Radley, Margaret Yorke, Celia Fremlin, Lawrence Block's Burglar series, et al. Anyone not familiar with their work is probably not on the same wave length. Manuscripts should be 50,000-80,000 words."

REEL MURDERS
MOVIE REVIEWS by Walter Albert

Forced Vengeance (1982). Director: James Fargo. Cast: Chuck Norris, David Opatoshu

The Wrong Box (1966). Director: Bryan Forbes. Script: Larry Gelbart & Burt Shrevelove. Music: John Barry. Cast: Michael Caine, Ralph Richardson, John Mills, Dudley Moore, Peter Cook, Wilfred Lawson, Nanette Newman.

Fog Island (1945). Director: Terry Morse. Cast: George Zucco, Lionel Atwill, Jerome Cowan, and Veda Ann Borg.

The Ruling Class (1972). Director: Peter Medak. Cast: Peter O'Toole, Arthur Lowe, Alastair Sim, Coral Browne, Nigel Green, Harry Andrews.

The Hills Have Eyes (1977). Director: Wes Craven

At the end of the Chuck Norris martial arts thriller **Forced Vengeance**, the leader of a special crime task force comments to Norris that there are "bodies all over the place; you're a real litter bug". This is probably the most memorable line in a film whose dialogue is the least of its virtues and is an apt comment on the number of corpses that Norris--and others—leave for uncredited flunkies to cart away. I don't think that I have ever been so aware in a Norris film of the many, and ugly, faces of death: hanging, semi-decapitation by a shard of glass, rape and strangulation, shooting, kicking, and knife-throwing. Norris is the adopted son of a family headed by a Jewish patriarch and security chief at their Hong Kong gambling casino, "The Lotus Dragon". The murders of his benefactor and son, his girl friend and best friend (a Jew, a Chinese-American, a blond, and a Black, an international array in keeping with the spirit of liberal brotherhood that characterizes the Norris productions) precipitate him into a spiraling conspiracy that eventually brings him into confrontation with the aged Chinese patriarch who is the mastermind of Osiris, the organization that order the murders. The Chinese patriarch, surprised watching an MGM Tom and Jerry cartoon in his villa, urges on his brutal bodyguard with excited commands to "kill him, kill him". Things are set right, I suppose, when the patriarch goes mad after the murder of his son, but some thoughtful viewers may wonder about the relationship between the violence in the cartoon and the film.

Norris' character is his usual, deceptively simple, moralistic persona, but he is so busy taking care of the forces arrayed against him that I missed those quiet moments that usually give some respite from the violence. After a bit my attention began to wander, and I found myself wondering how tall he really is and if he developed his formidable martial arts skills to pay back all the bullies who used to make life miserable for him in grammar school. That made me feel a bit better about all the killings since I have, over the years, had fantasies about paying back some of the bullies who made recess at Robert E. Lee Elementary School a nightmare. I had some difficulty converting the school yard into the setting of **Forced Vengeance**, and by the end of the film I had had my fill of violence and intermittently salubrious catharsis of this slick, bloody film.

Thanks to my remote control gadget, a somewhat earlier starting time, and frequent commercials, I was also able to watch most of a quite different film, **The Black Box**, a movie graced by the beetle-like humor of Dudley Moore and a perfect caricature of a fact-spouting pedant, played by Ralph Richardson. This 1966 British film was not as good as the sum of its parts, and was not particularly enhanced by a romantic subplot involving Michael Caine and a forgettable British actress, but the manic attempts of two members of the inimitable "Beyond the Fringe" company, Moore and Peter Cook, to make certain that their uncle, played by Richardson, is the last surviving member of a "tontine" and, thus, inheritor of a fortune of some one hundred thousand pounds, are often very funny. Cook is the fast-talking, "brains" of the team, constantly maneuvering around the sweet-natured bumbling of overactive Lothario Moore, but Moore gets the best line. After it is pointed out that Cook has altered a death certificate but inadvertently put on the next days' date, Moore comments, "here today, gone tomorrow," a perfectly logical statement in the context of this zany Victorian comedy. It is one of the few films I have seen in which the line "the butler did it" is uttered to truly comic effect, and the final scene is a triumph of comic miscalculations that somehow seem inevitable and right. A funny take-off on caper-and-chase films, **The Black Box** did not find much of an audience in this country in its original release and is sometimes hampered by a too-obvious and arch adaptation of the Robert Louis Stevenson original story by the American scriptwriters, but the talented cast surmounts most of the weaknesses and the film is worth watching for in the TV schedule.

I also saw a bit of **Fog Island**, a 1945 melodrama with Lionel Atwill and George Zucco, that involves an elaborate trap set by Zucco for the guests summoned to his island hideaway and detained for a night during which he intends to exact vengeance for an old betrayal and a prison term. There is an organ keyboard that controls a secret panel, a secret basement room rigged to imprison intruders and drown them, and a vast, vaulted living room ideally suited to long shots punctuated by moody silence filled with overly insistent music. If this film had not started at 2 a.m. after a showing of **Bullitt** that I had caught on the 11:30 late show just after I got home from my first viewing of the remarkable **The Ruling Class** in a decade, I might have been more in better shape to stay up and revel in the antiquated theatrics of **Fog Island**. As it was, I saw just enough to whet my appetite for more before, in the inimitable jargon of my children and their friends, I crashed for the night.

If **The Black Box** has not become a cult favorite locally at the Playhouse repertory theater, **The Ruling Class** turns up at least once a year. This funny, savage denunciation of the patriotic complacencies and reactionary politics of the "always an England" mystique may appeal more to anglophobes than to anglophiles, but the satire is so accurate and the acting so finely tuned to certain English stereotypes that much of the film is an acutely funny and exhilarating dissection of English eccentricities. The use of music-hall routines to comment on the stolidity of the upper classes and the brilliant performance by Arthur Lowe of the proper butler who, on inheriting 30,000 pounds, displays an enormous capacity for revolutionary comments on the system is in the best tradition of classical comedy. But this unconventional comedy is wedded to a much darker text with that particular genius the English have always had for mixing comedy and tragedy. Peter O'Toole plays the "moon loony" eldest surviving son who assumes the family title when his father is inadvertently hanged during some routine sex play in his room before dinner. O'Toole, believing himself to be Jesus Christ, returns from the asylum where he has been living in seclusion for some years. He preaches a gospel of love, which, as you can imagine, is somewhat upsetting to the British upper classes, who equate love with lust and who hunger after higher things like privilege and money. His family succeeds in marrying him off to a "lady" of dubious reputation, but he thwarts their plans to have recommitted by recovering his sanity. Unfortunately, his new lucidity reveals to him the corrupt, lewd reality of the society in which he lives, and the peaceful, non-violent Christ is replaced by a dark-dressed, stern puritan whose excessive rejection of sex masks "Jacks's" identification with Jack the Ripper. The satirical, funny tone of the film is rent savagely by two brutal murders each of which is followed by a terrifying scream that O'Toole modulates with such mastery that these moments are unforgettable theatrical experiences. O'Toole dominates the film, even against the competition of Alastair Sim (playing a frightened cleric who wears lavender robes under his more sober outer garment) and the accomplished acting of Coral Browne, Harry Andrews and Nigel Green. I shall not soon forget O'Toole's anguished cries toward the end of the film and a scene of seduction, between O'Toole and his selected bride, which they play as an oddly touching gambol with bird-like chirps and movements. In short, an original and highly recommendable film.

In order not to end on too sublime a note, I should like to mention a rather different mixture of violence and terror, Wes Craven's **The Hills Have Eyes**, in which a vacationing family heads off, against the advice of a desert rat, to look for a silver mine. Instead, they invade the territory of a mutant family that besieges and methodically begins to kill them. Wes Craven is better known as the director of the controversial **Last House on the Left** (which I have never seen), but the **Hills**, in comparison with **Forced Vengeance**, is almost tame and the low-budget look of this black and white film makes it seem closer to the post-atom bomb films of the unstylish fifties. More recently, Craven has directed **Deadly Blessing** which is a variation on his favorite theme of the intrusion by outsiders into a closed community. This has an attractive score by James Horner, a strong performance by Ernest Borgnine as a commune patriarch, and some handsome photography that suggest a larger budget. Unfortunately this film seems not to have had the hoped-for reception, and I am not aware of any more recent work by this director. Craven and Tobe Hooper (of **The Texas Chainsaw Massacre** and **Funhouse** were two of the more promising genre directors of the 70s but either their careers have not been, so far, commensurate with their talents or their talents were too circumscribed by their early work. Hooper was, of course, the director of the Steven Spielberg production of **Poltergeist**, but the success of this splendid ghost story was generally and, I believe, incorrectly credited to Spielberg's work rather than Hooper's. I find the work of both these directors to be of some interest, and I would like to think that by my somewhat pessimistic comments on their recent work will be answered shortly by the release of films that meet both critical and popular acclaim.

VERDICTS
Book Reviews

Robert Barnard. **The Case of the Missing Bronte.** Scribners, 1983, $11.95.

The discovery of a previously unknown book by one of the Bronte's is surely enough cause for excitement and envy in the literary and academic world. It would also be worth a sizable chunk of money to collectors and certain prestige-seeking universities (although I doubt that one million dollars is accurate). Since Supt. Perry Trthowan and his wife Jan are literate upper-class people, they are interested in the manuscript when introduced to it at a small village pub in Hutton-le-Dales.

Soon after, however, the owner, Mrs. Edith Wing, is attacked and the manuscript stolen. Other attacks occur, sinister Swedes appear (and perform an especially nasty piece of torture on Perry), librarians, teachers, and nefarious preachers almost fall over each other in their search for the missing Bronte. Eventually the papers are recovered and some semblance of order is restored, but not without Barnard's sharp wit and style being leveled at academia and bogus religion.

Unfortunately there are a few flaws in **The Missing Bronte**. For one thing, there is no murder. It is difficult to believe a Scotland Yard superintendent would be allowed to extensively investigate a few muggings and search for an old manuscript--regardless of how much he was personally interested. Second, Perry's first person narrative was a bit restrictive, not allowing Barnard's sarcasm and devastating insight to come through. On the other hand Perry's wife was shown as much more of a live person than ever before. **Bronte** may be one of Barnard's weaker efforts, but he is still an expert craftsman and a fascinating writer. His books should always be read before any other new offering. (Fred Dueren)

John Dickson Carr. **The Dead Sleep Lightly.** Doubleday, 1983, 181 pp., $11.95.

It was in 1932 that Dorothy L. Sayers, creatrix of Lord Peter Wimsey, wrote a piece for the London **Times** in praise of the latest mystery novel by a young American expatriate named John Dickson Carr. "Mr. Carr," she said, "can lead us away from the small, artificial, brightly-lit stage of the ordinary detective plot into the menace of outer darkness. He can create atmosphere with an adjective, and make a picture from a wet railing, a dusty table, a gas lamp blurred by the fog. He can alarm with an allusion or delight with a rollicking absurdity. In short, he can write...in the sense that every sentence gives a thrill of positive pleasure."

These words capture perfectly the essence of Carr's appeal both then when he was in his mid-twenties and today six years after his death. We may laugh at the legion of outlandish devices for committing murders under locked-room conditions with which he gifted his criminals. We may smile at those marvelously larger-than-life detective characters, Dr. Gideon Fell and Sir Henry Merrivale (modeled respectively after G.K. Chesterton and Winston Churchill). But when Carr evokes on the page the miasma of Gothic horror in the tradition of Poe and Ambrose Bierce, we shake with fright, and when he does one of his Robert Louis Stevenson high-adventure numbers we jump with excitement.

In 1939 Carr began writing radio plays for the BBC, then returned to the United States and worked for CBS on the new series called **Suspense** which chilled millions of listeners during its twenty year network run. After several months writing weekly **Suspense** dramas with titles like "Menace in Wax", "The Phantom Archer" and "The Man Without a Body", Carr went back to England and the BBC, which broadcast both new Carr scripts and revised versions of his **Suspense** work on a new and extremely popular series called **Appointment with Fear**.

The best of Carr's radio plays are as chilling and intellectually exciting as his finest novels, but his scripts have eluded publication in book form until now. This selection of nine dramas from **Appointment with Fear** we owe to Douglas G. Greene, history professor at Virginia's Old Dominion University and dedicated Carr Scholar, whose superbly informed introductory essay will orient even the neophyte reader to Carr's contributions to radio. "The Villa of the Damned" with which the collection closes is rather weak, but all the others—and especially the title play, "The Black Minute", "The Devil's Saint", and "The Dragon in the Pool"—display Carr the radio writer at atmospheric best. Here, for example, is the sinister Count Kohary in "The Devil's Saint", intruding on a masked ball in Paris of 1927 to play cat-and-mouse with the young Englishman who wants to marry the count's demon-haunted niece:

> KOHARY: ....Look there! Look all about us! Crowds of our fellow-guests, pouring down the main staircase. Shapes of nightmare. Shapes of delirium. Great goblin masks where only the eyes move. Mightn't you be terrified if you could look inside those painted masks to the real faces they hide?
> WHITEFORD: No, I don't think so. They're only ordinary people like ourselves.
> KOHARY: That, sir, is where you make your mistake. I shall expect you for the weekend.

That is Carr's magic at work. He made the transition from writing to spoken word with phenomenal success, creating atmosphere with an adjective and leading us into the outer darkness as chillingly as in his novels. Let us hope that **The Dead Sleep Lightly** is only the first collection of many. (Francis M. Nevins, Jr.)

Michael Hardwick. **The Private Life of Doctor Watson**. Dutton, 1983, 298 pp., $13.95.

Michael Hardwick has written a very authoritative autobiography of Dr. James Watson, companion and self-styled Boswell of Sherlock Holmes. An autobiography that I suspect will be, to a degree, quite controversial among those that go in for this sort of thing. It is more

fodder for the 'Canon' of Sherlockian discussion.
Sherlockian scholars have always wondered what happened to Watson's bullpup; just where his war wounds actually were; and why he kept an unframed portrait of Henry Ward Beecher. Michael Hardwick answers these questions and more.
The book covers the period of time from John's childhood until that fateful day in 1881 when he met his fellow lodger. The picture that Hardwick paints of Watson in the last few weeks before that monumental introduction ties in perfectly with the John Watson we meet in the beginning of A Study in Scarlet.
The book itself (like Hardwick's other Holmesian works), reads well. At times I almost believed that I was actually reading a non-fiction work. The parts dealing with his own family (father and brother) are especially satisfying. There is an interesting bit with the famous watch from The Sign of the Four. This is just one instance of the weaving together of the admittedly sparce clues provided by Dr. Doyle into a fabric of quality and believability.
The weakest parts of the narrative occur with the exhibition of what I call 'Meyer Syndrome'; namely the idea of 'Watson meets Beecher', 'Watson meets Bernhardt', in the manner first used by Nicholas Meyer in his two Holmes novels of the mid '70's. Watson's pursuit of anything in skirts takes up a good deal of the manuscript. This seems to be totally incongruous to the gallant Watson of The Sign of the Four, experience of the fair sex on three continents not withstanding.
On the whole, this is a stronger effort than Michael Harrison's autobiography of Holmes penned several years ago. Watson is a much more sympathetic character, and, of course, a better writer. I may turn into a Watsonian as a result of reading this book. My only question is, could we have been worshipping the wrong half of this famous tandem all these years? (Alan S. Mosier)

Mickey Spillane. **The Ship that Never Was.** Bantam, 1982, $1.95.

Mickey Spillane is an institution, famous for hard-boiled detective Mike Hammer, superspy Tiger Mann, and the tough-as-nails Dogeron Kelly. Although his books have sold more than 160 million copies world-wide, he hasn't published a book for the adult market since **The Last Cop Out** in 1973. Still, Spillane has been writing during this nine-year period. During the interim Spillane has published adventure stories for the young adult market, although one suspects that more adults buy these books than do younger readers.
The Ship that Never Was is Spillane's second novel for young adults. Larry Damar and Josh Toomey—the two young heroes that he introduced in **The Day the Sea Rolled Back**—discover the longboat from the H.M.S. **Tiger**, a British warship built in 1791. It's in perfect shape and has an old man in it who speaks a foreign language. Larry and Josh, together with their cooperative fathers Vincent Damar and Tim Toomey, soon discover that the old man, Vali Steptur, is the descendent of the exiled rulers of the European country Grandau, which was overrun by brigands and is still controlled by present day communists. Vali tells them that Grandau's true ruler is living on a supposedly deserted island, longing to return to her native land.
What follows is a wildly improbable tale in the true Spillane tradition which does not quite survive formal analysis but is nevertheless an exciting and entertaining story. The tale pits Josh and Larry against nefarious spies and an attacking submarine; it shows a hint of romance between Larry and Tila, the true heir to the Grandau throne; and it blends the romanticism of the sea saga with the action and adventure of

the spy thriller.
Amid the recurring rumors of a new Mike Hammer novel, Spillane has produced another worthy young adult adventure story which he claims originated in a challenge that he could not write a story which did not contain sex, violence, and bad language. Considering that he began his career writing comic book stories for just this market, such a challenge was ill advised. The action of the story is so tightly presented, the pacing so craftsmanlike, that the story works well and can be highly recommended for its intended market and the adult reader as well. (Jim Traylor)

Jon Tuska and Vicki Piekarski. **Encyclopedia of Frontier and Western Fiction.** McGraw-Hill, 1983, 365 pp., $29.95.

The Western as a fiction genre is one step from Boot Hill. All the classic shoot-em-up writers except 75-year-old Louis L'Amour are dead or in retirement, and most of today's so-called Westerns are exercises in sadism or pornography with a few perfunctory cowboy trimmings. it's a disastrous time for lovers of the genre but a propitious moment for a summing up of what was a staple in Americans' reading diet for generations.

In his preface to this encyclopedia, Jon Tuska subdivides all Western fiction into three categories. Historical reconstructions are those novels and stories that are factually accurate and primarily concerned with Westerners' interactions with the land, the Indians or each other. Those works that are true to history but built on mythical or ideological storylines he calls romantic historical reconstructions, and those that are factually unreliable and/or stereotyped as to plots and characters he labels as formulary works. If the encyclopedia were to be judged by its conceptual framework alone, it wouldn't get off lightly. The weighty intellectual tone which is so incongruous in a book about shoot-em-ups becomes even sillier when, amid quotations from Quintilian and Jung, the editors screw up the simplest Latin phrases (**in media res, magnum cum laude**) and invent some rules of copyright law which are roughly on a level with attributing the Leatherstocking Saga to Zane Grey. What saves the book is that most of its contents subverts its declared philosophy and reflects the knowledge and enthusiasm of a number of commentators who first and foremost like Westerns.

Each of more than two hundred alphabetical entries provides basic facts about an author's life, tersely evaluates his or her writings, and lists all the Westerns the person published plus all the movies based on them. One by one the horsemen pass by---shoot-em-up superstars like Max Brand and Zane Grey, enduring professionals like Harry Sinclair Drago and Ernest Haycox and Luke Short, mainstream writers like Mark Twain and Willa Cather and John Steinbeck. Trust Tuska and Piekarski to include everyone with some claim to literary significance who wrote anything remotely resembling a Western. Other entries deal with non-writers like Theodore Roosevelt and Frederic Remington who contributed to our image of the West, and with large subjects such as historical personalities, Native Americans, and women on the frontier.

No review can capture the variety of this or any encyclopedia, but perhaps a few awards in the style of a Warner Wolf sports wrapup will help. On the basis of this book, the prize for Strangest Biographical Fact goes to Max Brand, for asking Carl Jung to psychoanalyze him and getting turned down. The trophy for Weirdest Climax in a Western belongs to German author Karl May, in one of whose novels a dying Indian "acknowledges Christ and requests that an Ave Maria be sung for him". A Poor Proofreading award to Louis

L'Amour's **The Iron Marshall** which boasts (a) a character who's called Bert on one page and Hank a few pages later, (b) a "lean, wiry old man" whose age turns out to be 29, and (c) a buckaroo who unaccountably breaks into Swedish dialect for one and only one patch of conversation. And a booby prize goes to A. Leslie Scott, whose 125 virtually identical Texas Ranger novels are demolished in one magnificent paragraph worthy of John Simon. Joys like these punctuate the more sober and workmanlike encyclopedia entries on dozens of other Western writers.

The book is far from perfect either historically or grammatically. There are too many blunders like the reference to an ancestor of Zane Grey who, we are told, came to America with William Penn in 1682 and also defended Fort William Henry during the Revolutionary War. Every so often one is smacked on the nose by a botched sentence like this one on James Fenimore Cooper: "Adding the Fenimore to his name in 1826 in an unsuccessful attempt to inherit some land, the founder of American frontier fiction was born at Burlington, New Jersey." But by and large this is a highly readable and informative survey, offering food for thought and tons of fun for those who groove on the fiction of the American frontier. (Francis M. Nevins, Jr.)

James Fenimore Cooper. **The Ways of the Hour.** Putnam, 1850.

Cooper is frequently cited in histories of mystery and detective fiction for pioneering espionage fiction in **The Spy** (1821) and for including backwoodsy deductions in some of his Leatherstocking novels. But this early whodunit, published a mere nine years after Poe's "The Murders in the Rue Morgue", has been surprisingly ignored in most accounts of the **genre's** beginnings.

Admittedly, Cooper is more interested in making social and political points here than in telling a fast-paced story. His characters have long, erudite discussions about the controversies of the day--women's rights and roles (Cooper was no feminist), slavery (the main character is all for it!), capital punishment (one character remarks that "this country...could much better get along without preaching than without hanging"), and trial by press. The last-named issue is related to the author's main theme: an attack on the jury system, which the elitist Cooper believed could not produce real justice.

The talk is fascinating, despite (or because of?) some viewpoints that will appall contemporary readers. But Cooper had a good story to tell as well, a story that under all the nineteenth-century verbiage is not so different in structure and appeal from that of many more recent legal and mystery novels.

In the town of Biberry, Duke's County, New York, young Mary Monson (an assumed name concealing an Unspeakable Secret) is charged with arson and murder. Two charred skeletons have been found in the burned house of Peter and Dorothy Goodwin, with whom Mary had been living. Since the couple are missing, the natural conclusion is that they are the two victims, but one medical expert believes the skeletons belong to two women. The science of pathology is not advanced enough for anyone to say for sure. Lawyer Tom Dunscomb appears for the defense. The courtroom action, including an account of jury selection (driving home Cooper's point), is excellently done. The surprise solution, when it arrives, is of a kind that most disappoints experienced mystery readers, but it can be forgiven in a pioneering novel. What may have prevented **The Ways of the Hour** from recognition by historians as an early detective story is the lack of a central detective character, but surely detecting does go on, easily enough to qualify it as a detective novel in the present-day market. Be warned that this is anything but a great novel, partly because most of the characters are only fully fleshed enough to serve their functions in plot and debate. The book is, however, remarkable as a reflection of its times, and it does deserve to be noted as an early specimen of the Big Trial Novel. (Jon L. Breen)

Michael Underwood. **A Party to Murder.** St. Martin's, 1984, $10.95.

In a thirty-year career Underwood has employed a number of series characters. Scotland Yard detective Simon Manton, featured in his early novels, is fairly colorless and is relegated to a bit player in some books. Barrister Martin Ainsworth recurs in several books in major and minor roles. Nick and Clare Atwell, a cop-and-wife team, appear not too memorably in several novels of the late seventies. But Underwood's most interesting series sleuth is his current one, diminutive London solicitor Rosa Epton, who makes her fourth appearance in **A Party to Murder.**

Some of the staff of the Chief Prosecuting Solicitor's office in the town of Grainfield are less than happy with their newly-appointed chief, Murray Riston. When previously a member of the staff, Riston has an affair with colleague Caroline Allard and treated her shabbily. Also, he is rumored to have unethically protected from criminal proceedings locally powerful Rex Kline, now his father-in-law. Long-time deputy Charles Buck, who wrongly believes outgoing chief Edward Patching supported his own candidacy, is especially upset at the appointment and greats Riston with unconcealed hostility. At the annual Christmas office party, things come to a head in murder. The victim, though, is not Riston but staff member Tom Hunsey, an incompetent and indecisive gossip-monger who is an embarrassment (albeit a seemingly harmless one) to his colleagues.

Caroline, the main suspect, is the kind of weak-kneed sad sack that the unjustly accused tend to be in Underwood's novels, but she has the good sense to call in her law school classmate Rosa, who solves the case efficiently. (All the clues, unfortunately, are not made known to the reader.) Rosa briefs Michael Ainsworth to expose the real killer (both surprising and credible) in court, Perry Mason fashion.

Through his career, Underwood has always been reliable and seldom brilliant, but his most recent books are among his best. (Jon L. Breen)

Joseph Hansen. **Backtrack.** Penguin Books, 1983, 167 pp.

This short thriller is set in Hansen territory, sensual southern California, and stocked with Hansen Cast, extraordinary people who are being persuaded to seem ordinary.

Alan Tarr, an eighteen-year old off to seek knowledge of his recently deceased father and possibly to avenge his death, tells the story in "then" and "now" sections. Eric Tarr had left his wife and infant son years ago for a male lover and a movie career--and those desires were not the worst of his trangressions. As is established in the first paragraph, Alan has found out the painful way that he may already have found out too much.

The tale is slight in plot but rich in suspense and imagery. The danger and simplicity of the beaches, canyons, wind, and moonlight compare with the rugged gentleness of the main characters. The effect is satisfying. (Martha Alderson)

Joseph Hansen. **Nightwork**. Holt, Rinehart and Winston, 1984, 172 pp.

Nightwork is the unpleasant, high-paying, off-hours work people do out of desperation to make good money and in exchange for not asking too many questions. There are a lot of reasons, though, why an insurance company might not pay benefits to a client's family when the client died during nightwork. Dave Brandstetter investigates the circumstances to determine whether the company should pay, and he investigates the nightwork itself, of course.

Hansen's Los Angeles images are superb as usual, and the tension builds until the last moment.

This seventh Dave Brandstetter mystery is a tribute to the author's friendship with his protagonist. Brandstetter, now a free-lance death claims insurance investigator, is very real but no longer self-conscious. He doggedly carries out his work. He fully appreciates his lover/companion/associate, Cecil Harris. He cares deeply about his father's young widow, Amanda Brandstetter. He does all within his power to see that justice is done for those he meets—the white bigoted plodders, the leaders and members of the small black church, the aged invalid tranvestite land owner. That's Dave Brandstetter, just being the best kind of insurance investigator he can be.

The realism of this novel means that Dave cannot right all the wrongs. Progressive industrialization and greed have wrought horrors that will continue for generations. Several loose ends remain tangled, yet the mystery is solved. Dave Brandstetter is a believable hero. (Martha Alderson)

Joe Hyams. **Murder at the Academy Awards**. St. Martin's, 1983, 182 pp., $11.95.

Hollywood is supposed to be exciting, what with its glamour mentality and shallow virtues. Joe Hyams describes a Hollywood full of vainglorious people, where ambition is the over-riding force of forces. His Hollywood is stereo-typical; schĕming producers, effeminate directors, and gratuitous sex.

Hyams creates two detectives in the LAPD, a man and a woman, and their affairs entangle them in a situation where it is difficult to separate work from play. These two are mildly interesting, but Hyams characters seem to lack anything to suggest that they are indeed, living, breathing people. Perhaps plastic people are as much a part of the Hollywood mystique as the artificial coloring mentioned above.

Detectives "Punch" Roberts and Bonny Cutler narrow down the suspects with the help of a retired gossip columnist, but the reader is never much in doubt as to who is the actual culprit.

This early realization factor is the major weakness of the book. I kept waiting for the plot twist that never came.

Briefly, Eva Johnson is murdered by a digestible bomb while accepting the Oscar for best picture, won by a rigged vote. All the suspects are, of course, in the vicinity at the time. Politics becomes the eventual solution and once the topic arises, all is clear to the reader, if not the detectives.

Author Joe Hyams predominant crime is obviousness. (Alan S. Mosier)

S.T. Haymon. **Death and the Pregnant Virgin**. St. Martin's, 1980, Bantam, 1984.

The village of Mauthen Barbary is crowded with a special kind of tourist, couples who are anxious to conceive children. They have come to celebrate the anniversary of the finding of the "Lady of Promise", a carved wooden figure of a pregnant woman, presumably a primitive fertility figure. The carving is at least life-size and is kept in a large building, made to be it's shrine. It's discoverer, old Charles Griffin, has made something of a cult of it.

After the celebratory procession, the dead body of Rachel Cass, a 19 year-old girl with a reputation for purity and saintliness, is found in the shrine. Detective Inspector Ben Jurnet, on the scene by chance, sets to work on the problem. He is frustrated by the insistence of her brother, sister-in-law, and friends, that **no one** could possibly have had a motive for killing Rachel. But when the post-mortem shows that she was pregnant, though still technically a virgin, one motive is apparent. Then Griffin's dead body is found.

Jurnet peers into every corner, and listens carefully to what everyone says. He finds an excellent motive for both murders, and the culprit too. The detection is fine, the background interesting. I was, however, unamused to find that I was being asked to accept the likelihood of a miracle. (Maryell Cleary)

Antonia Fraser. **Cool Repentance.** Norton, 1982.

Fraser has created a prototypical "liberated woman" detective: young, gorgeous, sexy, glamorously at work in the glamorous television business, brainy, and very well-paid. She sports an expensive red suede jacket and a new, fast Mercedes sports car. She's all of these things, and I didn't like her. Jealousy? Maybe so....

In this book, her fourth, Jem is filming a local music and drama festival for a Megalith TV series. The festival becomes a major attraction when Christabel Cartwright, who created a scandal when she ran off with a budding pop singer, "Iron Boy", comes back to her family and takes two parts in plays in the festival. She admits to Jemima that she is frightened and feels safest among many people. The first death occurs when all the television and festival people are having a picnic on the beach. A young and talented actress drowns while wearing Christabel's bathing costume; this is assumed to be an accident. Then the director of the plays is strangled, and there's no question of accident any more. Who and why are the questions.

The suspects include Julian, Christabel's complaisant husband; her two teen-aged daughters; her lover-not "Iron Boy", but an older one; the butler and cook, parents of "Iron Boy", who blame Christabel for taking him away; and Ketty, the cook's sister, who manages the household and is in love with Julian. It would be difficult for an experienced mystery reader to be truly surprised by the ending, but if you want your chances to be higher, don't read the review segments on the back of the dust jacket.

Someone tell me, if Jemima Shore is so smart, why can't she prevent a death or two? (Maryell Cleary)

Ellis Peters. **The Sanctuary Sparrow.** Morrow & Co., 1983.

Ellis Peters (Edith Pargeter) must be having fun writing the Brother Cafael series. She has created a convincing 12th century English city, Shrewsbury, and its neighboring abbey. Brother Cafael, the abbey's herbalist, is surely one of the most engaging of the newly-minted detectives. He is middle-aged, strong and intelligent, retired from years as a Crusader to a quiet life serving God and his fellows. He has known women, in the Biblical sense, and he is tender towards young love. His heart is as warm as his medicines are potent.

In this, the seventh, a poor young traveling jongleur seeks sanctuary in the abbey church, as he is being pursued by a mob of furious townsmen who accuse him of theft and murder. He had been entertaining at a wedding in Shrewsbury, was thrown out without his fee, and when the man of the house was found with his head bashed—not really dead, however—and his gold and silver gone, the youth is naturally suspected. It soon appears that Liliwin, the jongleur, had nothing to do with the crime, but Cafael has to solve it in the 40 days' time a person is allowed sanctuary. As usual, greed is punished and young love triumphs. But there is painful knowledge of what lack of concern for a human being can wreak, how it can warp and lead to death. Brother Cafael never leaves us without a moral, and a good thing, too. (Maryell Cleary)

Will Jacobs and Gerard Jones. **The Beaver Papers.** Crown Publishers, 1983.

The Beaver Papers is a brilliantly conceived and executed satire. As such, it would seemingly have no more appeal to the mystery fan than any other well-done general satirical work.

However, the script treatment "Farewell, My Beaver", purportedly the work of Raymond Chandler, is a clever takeoff on private eyes, with "creepy" Eddie playing detective. I am not going to tell anyone that this 1/25th of the book is worth the price of admission, but you will probably like it.

You should also enjoy the title of Mickey Spillane's supposed submission (one of the many not published), even if you will have an easy time guessing the title. You should enjoy even more some of the other treatments; real familiarity with the **Leave It to Beaver** TV series is not necessary. Perhaps, instead of buying a copy, you should do what I did and borrow one from a friend. (Jeff Banks)

James Crumley. **Dancing Bear.** Random House, 1983, $12.95.

Dancing Bear is another detective adventure of the "wilderness private eye" Milo Milodragovitch. More importantly, it is a return to the fine form of **The Wrong Case**, in which Milo made his memorable debut. Milo encounters an old lover of his long-dead dad, and she asks him (glossing over his long retirement) to do a private investigation for her "to satisfy a nosy old woman". Naturally, he accepts the case, despite a lovely initial reaction to the letter inviting him to stop by:

> And the phrase 'a case'...My god, even when I worked for myself, I never got cases; the sort of work I did came in crocks (p. 12).

Naturally, the job turns out to be much more (and much more dangerous) than it seemed at first. He finds himself hunted by a vicious ring of poachers—who turn out finally to be something infinitely more sinister. He acquires an assistant that is not quite a bungler, but is completely unpredictable (a Vietnam vet whose mind has come thoroughly unhinged). The assistant tells him a really delightful "North Dakota Joke" (the Montana equivalent of a Polack Joke, which in Texas would be an Aggie Joke) that won't get retold here out of context,

because it is worth the price of the book, and I hope everyone who reads this will rush out and buy one.
The joke is to be found on page 179, and somewhere (sorry, I lost my page reference on this) there is a lovely insight from the perspective of a detective on we humans:

> I was surprised to find out how few strangers, when I watched their lives for a few days, turned out to be perfectly boring. Almost everyone, it seemed, had at least one secret life. Except me. I was the watcher, the uninvolved observer.

There is enough violence for a Dashiell Hammett novel and my fellow Spillane fans will delight in the fact that the much-put-upon hero dishes out his share of it towards the end of the book. As with both Hammett and Spillane, the hero's violence is well motivated.
Finally, the mystery is solved, the villain put in his place, which may well be being built into a Toyota. The hero lays the worst of his ghosts, and renounces his profession (as well as his alcoholism) for what seems to be the final time. The reader meets a leavening of nice people along with the gaggle of very nasty ones he would normally expect.
Highly Recommended. (Jeff Banks)

Matthew J. Bruccoli. **Ross Macdonald**. Harcourt, Brace, Jovanovich, 1984.

This is the first biography of Ross Macdonald/Kenneth Millar (just Ross Macdonald to me) that I know of, and is, according to the dust jacket, the first of an "HBJ Album Biographies" series, edited by Mr. Bruccoli. The series is purported to provide "generously illustrated and compact yet thorough studies of modern American writers, intended primarily for readers who may not be familiar with the fuller biographies". Its contents are a three page chronology, a two page introduction, 119 pages of biography, notes, a selected bibliography and an index. Fully 41 of those 119 pages, however, are taken up by photographs, leaving 78 pages of text for your $14.95. Apparently, devoting a third of the biography to photos is what distinguishes this work as an "album biography". Many of those photographs are interesting ones of Macdonald, but many of those were, very irritating to me, undated. Most of the photos were devoted to printed material: photos of dust jackets, manuscript pages, paperback covers, movie posters and the like. And, there were several photos, posed, of other authors. In my opinion this whole collection was very unsatisfactory, and added up to revealing little about Macdonald. The biography portion of the formula was, however, the big disappointment. When I finished it, I had to check to make sure it even claimed to be a biography. It did.. The dust jacket informed me that "the depth of [Bruccoli's] vision and the precision of his research establish standards for the literary biography". What those standards are is another matter. His "vision" consists mainly of a series of plot summaries of Macdonald books along with some brief and superficial critical commentary by himself and occasional quotations from contemporaneous reviews. Much better material along these lines can be found in the studies by Jerry Spier and, especially, Peter Wolfe. Between these plot summaries are sandwiched miniscule and unsatisfying details of the course of Macdonald's life. Of course, Bruccoli is down to about twenty pages of biography by now and he is unable to give the reader any sort of feeling for the real like person behind the few facts he conveys. This is a book that left me feeling sad. It ends with the fact that Ross Macdonald died in July, 1983, but with nothing to take from it to remember him by. I think I will pick up one of the Lew Archer novels to give me a more nourishing and palatable remembrance, and I hope that someone is out there writing something better than this cut and paste scrapbook biography. (David Grothe)

Anne Morice. **Murder by Proxy.** St. Martin's, 1978.

The title of this novel gives a decided clue to the indirectness of murder within. The names of the characters in the novel provide another blatant set of clues to some of the developments. It seems, however, that even the most Anglophile mystery readers miss the latter set of clues.

An earthy, self-centered landowner named Harry has provided for his estranged wife Catherine and their daughter Mary by giving them a house on his property and near his own house. Harry lives now with Anne who seems to have possession of Harry's affection by being common-law wife but who is not satisfied with her lot because of lack of legal status, pervasive jealousy, and fear for her life. Harry and Anne's small daughter is Lizzie, but Anne claims to be pregnant with Harry's son. A friend involved in the family affairs is Jane, and her frequent companion Tom gives Harry financial advice and is his good buddy. Does any of this sound familiar to English Literature students? I have to admit to much head pounding when the author pointed out the use of these Tudor analogies. (Morice explained that this was the only time she set out to construct a story around a predetermined plot.) Morice's series character, Tessa Crichton, is called in by her old school chum Anne of Harry-and-Anne and performs in her usually competent and cheeky way.

Murder by Proxy is worth rereading to catch the humorous undercurrent of the history allusions. (Martha Alderson)

Anne Morice. **Murder Post-dated.** London: MacMillan, 1983, 192 pp.

The familiar antics of actress Theresa (Tessa) Crichton return. In fact, a lot of familiar Morice characters appear in this novel. Tessa is nosy and energetic as usual (perhaps somewhat less abrasive). Her eccentric cousin, playwright Toby Crichton, is as cantankerous and lovable as ever. Her husband, Robin Price of Scotland Yard, is as charming but distant as ever. And Ellen, the perfect young cousin, returns after a several book vacation. It doesn't matter to the structure of the novel whether these family members are familiar or not, but Morice fans will enjoy the reunion.

There are several other reappearances. Most of the cast from **Hollow Vengeance** (1981) have active parts. Marc Carrington is engaged again and to another young woman who has a peculiar personality and who is the center of tragedy. Neighbors, friends, and family nearly fill the list. But in Morice novels, close associates of the protagonist are frequently victims or murderers. It is not necessarily so, though; so the reader must beware of expecting a formula solution.

The events are truly puzzling. A woman is missing with lots of signs pointing toward an untimely, violent end. Her husband's explanations shift as frequently as a kite in the wind. Young lovers break up and make up numerous times for confusing reasons. A fire makes a nightmare come true. Tessa and her friends and relatives and new acquaintances try to find some connections among or come to some conclusions about any of the events. There are clues, but they are nicely submerged in the frantic pace and very funny observations of the incorrigible Tessa. (Martha Alderson)

Ted Wood. **Dead in the Water.** Scribners, $11.95.
Don Flynn. **Murder isn't Enough.** Walker, $12.95.

In the past couple of years, two publishers noted for quality of British mysteries have brought glad tidings to American mystery fans and writers. Scribners has instituted an annual contest for new crime novelists, and Walker has expanded its list to include American authors as well as its standard line of imports.

Ted Wood, an accomplished Canadian playwright and magazine writer, takes the second Scribner Crime Novel Award, with a novel quite different from its predecessor, Carol Clemeau's **The Ariadne Clue,** and nearly as good. Reid Bennett, a Toronto policeman who left town after killing two bikers who were participating in a gang rape, is now the chief of police (and only human officer) of Murphy's Harbour, a tiny lakefront town. Helping him maintain law and order, not an onerous chore ordinarily, are a civilian assistant named Murphy, partially disabled with World War II injuries, and a reliable police dog named Sam. A Vietnam veteran who doesn't relish killing but is willing to do it in the line of duty, Bennett is a macho hero not far removed from Matt Helm, Travis McGee, or Spenser.

Suddenly police work in the little community becomes more demanding. A body is found in the lake. A local lodgekeeper, who was a wartime crony of Murphy's, has disappeared. The bike gang whose membership Bennett reduced in his Toronto days is sighted in the area. And a beautiful blonde with plenty to hide asks Bennett's help in finding her missing lover. With sound police procedure appropriate to a **very** small force, Bennett gradually gets to the truth. The action is plentiful, the first-person writing low-key and unself-conscious, and the solution fairly clued.

Don Flynn's first-person hero is Ed Fitzgerald, a New York **Tribune** rewrite man transferred to the courthouse beat when veteran legman (i.e., a reporter good at finding news but not at writing it) Sandy Pearl dies in a hit-run accident. Ed soon has reason to suspect Sandy was murdered, and when he starts to investigate turns up other bodies with disquieting frequency.

Fitzgerald is a likeable, self-deprecating character. Dogged and determined but given to making the wrong move at crucial times, possibly due to his years of vegetating on the rewrite desk, he is as far from the omniscient supersleuths of earlier days as could be imagined. His boss, known as Ironhead, is an irascible city editor in the grand tradition.

Flynn's first novel has a fine background of Manhattan journalism and jurisprudence and an intricate but comprehensible plot. But most important are the crisp style, the rapid pace, and the deft, economical characterization. (Jon L. Breen; these two reviews originally appeared in the **Los Angeles Federal Savings Quarterly,** Winter, 1984)

The Documents In the Case (Letters)

From Wm. F. Deeck:

I read Earl F. Bargainnier's article on "The Old Man in the Corner" with interest, but also with a great deal of despondency. Mr. Bargainnier says: "But surely someone can provide a list of all the stories as originally published in magazine form and then in their first collected form."

But does Mr. Bargainnier grant us the titles of the stories in the Dover edition and the IPL reprint? Of course not. And since my edition is neither one of these for **The Man In The Corner**, I've got a third factor to wrestle with.

The edition of **The Man In The Corner** that I possess is the 1966 W.W. Norton Seagull Library of Mystery and Suspense. This edition contains an introduction by Vincent Starrett, and, frankly, he might not have bothered for all the information it contains. I understand Starrett had his days, but the day he wrote this introduction was not one of them. Indeed, he does not even mention **The Case Of Miss Elliott**.

The W.W. Norton edition comprises the following stories: "The Fenchurch Street Mystery"; "The Robbery in Phillimore Terrace"; "The York Mystery"; "The Mysterious Death on the Underground Railway"; "The Theft at the English Provident Bank"; "The Dublin Mystery"; "The Regent's Park Murder"; "The De Genneville Peerage"; "The Mysterious Death in Percy Street"; "The Liverpool Mystery"; "The Edinburgh Mystery"; "An Unparalleled Outrage". At least I think those are the titles; the 36 chapters make the whole thing very confusing.

For **The Case Of Miss Elliott**, Barzun and Taylor list the following titles: "The Case of Miss Elliott"; "Tragedy in Dartmoor Terrace"; "Who Stole the Black Diamonds?"; "The Murder of Miss Pebmarsh"; "The Lisson Grove Mystery"; "The Mystery of Cigarette"; "The Tremarn Case"; "The Fate of the **Artemis**"; "The Disappearance of Count Collini"; "The Ayrsham Mystery"; "The Affair at the Novelty Theatre"; and, "The Tragedy of Barnsdale Manor".

Barzun and Taylor do not have a listing for **Unravelled Knots**, but they do say that it's a collection of thirteen stories. I'm willing to accept their count in this instance, even though they say about **The Man In The Corner** that the "thirty-six chapters serve to present about half that number of cases" and I can't get 12 as about half of 36.

Well, so far, if everyone—including me—has been on the ball, we have a total of 37. Throw in the "repressed" story, as Mr. Bargainnier describes it, and you come up with the speculated 38 stories.

Further titles, as listed in Hubin—and I am working from the mimeographed pages as published in TAD—**The Old Man in the Corner Unravels the Mystery of the Fulton Gardens Mystery, and the Moorland**

Tragedy; The Old Man in the Corner Unravels the Mystery of the Khaki Tunic; The Old Man in the Corner Unravels the Mystery of the Pearl Necklace, and The Tragedy in Bishops' Road; The Old Man in the Corner Unravels the Mystery of the Russian Prince, and of Dog's Tooth Cliff; The Old Man in the Corner Unravels the Mystery of the White Carnation, and the Montmarte Hat.
The above are listed in Hubin as books. Thus, if these are not duplicated in **Unravelled Knots**, you've got 47 stories, not 38. If they are indeed all in **Unravelled Knots**, we're still about three stories short, unless I lost track somewhere, which definitely possible. **[According to both the first and revised editions of Hubin, the 9 stories that Mr. Deeck lists above did indeed appear in Unravelled Knots.]**
All of this reminds me of the problems I have had with various editions of Roy Vickers' Department of Dead Ends stories. Someday I hope someone will straighten that out.
Now you can see why I believe most publishers are cretins. Much of the information they publish about their books is erroneous or incomplete, or they publish editions that bear little relation to other editions. I'd say a pox on all their houses, but then what would we do for reading and arguing material.

From E.F. Bleiler:

I was surprised to read Mr. Bargainnier's article about **The Old Man in the Corner**, for I had never heard of the International Polygonics editions of Orczy, nor of IPL, nor the Sparafuciles. I'll have to see if I can find a copy of their edition of **Lady Molly** just to see what else they say in their introduction.
Mr. Bargainnier raises a couple of points: the story titles, the age of the "old man", and (though he doesn't exactly raise the point), his identity.
The first and second series of stories about the Old Man appeared in the **Royal Magazine**, a British publication, as indicated:

"The Fenchurch Street Mystery" May 1901
"The Mystery in Phillimore Terrace" June 1901
"The Mysterious Death on the Underground Railway" July 1901
"The Theft at the English Provident Bank" August 1901
"The Regent's Park Murder" September 1901
"The Mysterious Death in Percy Street" October 1901

"The Glasgow Mystery" April 1902
"The York Mystery" May 1902
"The Liverpool Mystery" June 1902
"The Brighton Mystery" July 1902
"The Edinburgh Mystery" August 1902
"The Dublin Mystery" September 1902
"The Birmingham Mystery" October 1902

All these stories, except "the Glasgow Mystery", were reprinted in the Greening (London 1909) **The old Man in the Corner** and the Dodd, Mead (N.Y. 1909) **The Man in the Corner**, which are the same in content. The stories were rearranged somewhat, with "The Mysterious Death in Percy Street" placed last, for obvious reasons. To create the appearance of a novel (which the publishers thought would sell better than a collection of short stories), the individual stories were broken into parts, with separate chapter heads for each part. The first chapter head for each story was in most cases the original story title, although

"The Mysterious in Phillimore Terrace" became "The Robbery in Phillimore Terrace", "The Brighton Mystery" became "An Unparalleled Outrage", and "The Birmingham Mystery", "The De Genneville Peerage".
"The Glasgow Mystery" was not reprinted in these editions, for Baroness Orczy had made a serious legal error, flawing the story for a British (particularly Scottish) market. The Story was first published in book form in the Dover (1980) edition.
The third series of stories also appeared in the **Royal Magazine**:

"The Case of Miss Elliott" April 1904
"The Hocussing of Cigarette" May 1904
"The Tragedy in Dartmoor Terrace" June 1904
"Who Stole the Black Diamonds?" July 1904
"The Murder of Miss Pebmarsh" August 1904
"The Lisson Grove Mystery" September 1904
"The Tremarn Case" October 1904
"The Fate of the **Artemis**" November 1904
"The Disappearance of Count Collini" December 1904
"The Ayrsham Mystery" January 1905
"The Affair of the Novelty Theatre" February 1905
"The Tragedy of Barnsdale Manor" March 1905

The stories above were published in sequence in **The Case of Miss Elliott** (1905). Why they saw book publication before the first and second series is not known. A reasonable guess is that the stage success of **The Scarlet Pimpernel** called attention to material that was recent and fresh in memory, but there is no evidence, and this may be a wrong explanation.
The fourth and last series of stories is as follows:

"The Mystery of the Khaki Tunic"
"The Mystery of the Ingres Masterpiece"
"The Mystery of the Pearl Necklace"
"The Mystery of the Russian Prince"
"The Mysterious Tragedy in Bishop's Road"
"The Mystery of the Dog Tooth's Cliff"
"The Tytherton Case"
"The Mystery of Brudenell Court"
"The Mystery of the White Carnation"
"The Mystery of the Montmartre Hat"
"The Miser of Maida Vale"
"The Fulton Gardens Mystery"
"A Moorland Tragedy"

These were picked up in **Unravelled Knots** (1925). They had recently been published in periodical form in both Great Britain and the United States, but I am sorry to say that I cannot find my notes and don't trust my memory as to exact date and place.
These stories of the fourth series are frankly set in the period after World War I, and Orczy now refers to the detective (in her text) as the Old Man in the Corner, whereas in the previous three series he had been only the Man in the Corner. But then more than twenty years had passed since Miss Burton first met him. The series ends with the Old Man in flight once again, this time after a jewel robbery that he had committed. The consensus has been (and I agree with it) that these stories are not so good as the earlier ones, being a rather mechanical rehash of what had once been somewhat original.
On the questions of the identity and age of the (Old) Man in the Corner: I know that it is often stated, as has Mr. Bargainnier, that the

Old Man is not identified by name, this is not really correct. In the original final story, "The Mysterious Death in Percy Street", he is definitely named Owen, although his first name is not given. (Greening, p. 327; Dodd, Mead, p. 310; Dover, p. 35)

His age is more tricky. The fullest description of him appears in the first story, "so pale, so thin, with such funny light-coloured hair, brushed very smoothly across the top of a very obviously bald crown". This description suggests middle-age, although nowhere, so far as I could find, does Orczy commit herself as to age. In her text, for the first three series, she always refers to Owen only as the Man in the Corner. The periodical artist (P. B. Hickling) and the Greening-Dodd, Mead artist, (H. Brock), on the other hand, show Owen, undoubtedly with editorial approval, as an elderly man. I would guess that this difference of interpretation results from the unresolved contradiction in Orczy's concept of the detective-criminal: the man Owen cannot be very old, while the querulous, compulsive detective as a role should be elderly.

Another curious aspect of the stories is the attitude of Miss Mary Burton, the woman journalist who takes down the stories. Apparently an **Absence of Malice** type, she seems indifferent to justice and/or the law. Although she has good reason to believe that Owen murdered his aunt, she simply warns him and is quite prepared to resume the old relationship a generation later when she chances to meet him a teashop. Nor does she seem to disturbed when she learns that Owen has pulled off a massive diamond heist.

From Harald Mogensen:

In TMF (Nov.-Dec.1983) E. F. Bleiler reviews **Kriminallitteraturens Kalvakade. Kriminallitteraturen i billeder og tekst** (1983) by Tage la Cour and Harald Mogensen. Allow me to protest mildly. Bleiler is constantly comparing the work with **The Murder Book** (Danish edition 1969, English and American editions 1971) by the same authors. Nothing could be more wrong. It is completely new-written text. About 70 percent of the illustrations are new. The first book was thematically structured-whereas the latter one is chronologically structured. Bleiler calls it a coffee-table book, a kind of book that he does not like. But **Kriminallitteraturens Kalvakade** is not a coffee-table book. It belongs to the modern, effective and at the same time entertaining type--a popular culture book which pedagogically explains things by means of text as well as by illustrations with captions.

Bleiler uses two-thirds of his review enumerating some errors--and then adding: "But such errors are uncommon, and I should not nitpick". But it is **he** who is constantly nitpicking. He mentions that Ruth Rendell is only mentioned with two lines. She is, however, mentioned with 26 lines plus there is an illustration with a two-lined caption. I do not wish to nitpick his review of the book. But it is, however, incredible that he does not mention the fact that Dashiell Hammett and the hard-boiled American break-through has received the same amount of space in the book as Sir Arthur Conan Doyle. Two of the crime-genre's main characters-important innovators. In this book they are evaluated equally in the historic development of the genre. In the last but one survey **The Whodunit. An Informal History of Detective Fiction** (Collier Books, NY. 1981) by Benvenuti and Rizzoni--the American innovation is dealt with in al almost en passent manner. The original Italian work--the first edition did also contain colour-illustrations--has in the American edition lost this quality and appears in a black/white simplification. We do not wish such a fate. It seems quite impressive to us that a Danish publishing firm--Lademann--is able to publish such a

richly colour-illustrated book. A work of such high technical and design quality with the little Danish language area as a sales basis. We, the Danes, amount to 5,000,000 people inclusive Greenland and the Faroes islands towards west and Christiansoe islands towards east close to the Baltic coast of the Soviet Union.
Coffee-table book—oh, my foot....

From Walter and Jean Shine:

We continue to marvel at Art Scott's way with words. His analysis (7:6:32) of the Ken Darby book—we won't dignify it by mentioning its title for fear that repetition will somehow enhance its stature—uses scalpel and scythe, rapier, dagger, sabre and sword to hack away at one of the genre's most astounding and totally undeserved, egos. But even Art's terms ("disastrous", "arrogance", "stupidity", "pathetic", "wrong, wrong, wrong", "lacks sense", "lame imitation", "goes off the walls", "utterly false", ... "despicable", "sleazy", "egregious", "crap", "offensive abomination", "vile") fail to convey the mischief done by this half-man. But Art goes on and finds the perfect appellation when, mid-way in his dissection, he locates and describes the precise core of K.D.'s being by naming him "an obviously incandescent asshole". Hurrah and Hosanna to the highest for the art of Scott!

If Art doesn't know it, he and your readers **should** know that the same insufferable Rectum of Rectitude had the effrontery on a prior occasion to disgorge himself of his Birch Society bilge in the July, 1981 (#28) issue of the **JDM Bibliophile**. Without John D. MacDonald's leave, he forged Travis McGee's name to what purported to be an interchange between Travis and an unnamed correspondent, railing against the "Third Estate". (He meant the fourth Estate, of course, but what could you expect from one such as he?) No attempt was made to gainsay the implication, so the reader was left with the impression that JDM was the author of the Travis letter. We responded in the January, 1982 (#29) issue with a song-poem, but we're afraid it was beyond the ken of this Ken. Discomfiture and damnation to all such dopes!

And, Art, we'll make a small wager (say a dinner in Chicago next October) that the only thing you found to commend Knocked-Down KD for, the 8 pages of blueprints, were probably drawn for him by some graphics designer from his Hollywood clan.

From Teri White:

Just a couple of brief comments on the last issue. First, while i cannot speak for Melinda Reynolds (nor does she need me to, of course) for myself I take polite issue with Mr. Isaac's comment that both Ms. Reynolds and myself seem to have "read narrowly". I have read, over the last thirty or so years an average of 5-10 books a week and in that time, I dare say, have sampled most kinds of books, both within and without the genre. Even if I wanted to restrict myself to my favorites (PI, police procedural, psychological thrillers) it would be difficult to do so and still have enough to read. Let me just say that having tried all kinds of books, I now have certain favorites. Narrowly read? I don't think so.

I do owe Art Scott a debt for his remarks on **The Brownstone House of Nero Wolfe**. Without reading his comments, I might have simply picked up the book from the library shelf and taken it home. Instead, warned in advance, I browsed through the final section. It did not take long for me to decide that any mind which could spill such homophobic drivel onto the page would have nothing to say that would interest me. It amazes me that the gay population seems to be the last remaining group that is still acceptably spoken of in such terms. I suppose every society needs a group like that and now that racism and sexism against women are unfashionable, gays are easily attacked. At least I don't have to waste my time reading it.

From Bob Adey:

I very much enjoyed the latest two issues of TMF, and, if anything, I probably like the September/October issue the better of the two, not because it was academic in content, but because the articles were full of facts--abstruse facts maybe, but facts nonetheless. Two letters to comment on. William F. Deeck's because he lists amongst his superior novels two by one of my favourite authors, Joseph Harrington. Harrington wrote only three books, all top quality, and in my view probably the best police procedurals ever written—but very rarely do they get a mention, so all power to William Deeck's elbow.

Secondly Melinda Reynolds' Dick Francis checklist doesn't include Francis' contribution to a round robin short story published in Britain's TV Times (the one with details of our commercial channel programmes). Full details are: Chapter 1 of "The Diamonds are Forever Mystery" in the TV Times for July 12, 1973. The other three chapters, all in the same issue, came from Gavin Lyall, Miles Tripp and Christianna Brand.

From Marv Lachman:

I can't really agree with Fred Isaac in anything but his title. A lot of academic writers are "bleeding the fun out" of the mystery by their own boring writing and by the contortions they go through to make the mystery "significant". Trying to develop broader markets, as he suggests, seems unnecessary. Most mystery readers will continue to read and enjoy the books but will not read **about** the mystery. If they were going to do otherwise, TMF would have three thousand subscribers. The most realistic thing we can hope for is that the people who write **about** the mystery will try to entertain a bit more. As Bob Adey says in the latest issue, the trick is "to make the academic entertaining". Fortunately, there are many people around who can do that, e.g., Walter Albert, Dave Lewis, Greg Goode, Frank McSherry, Charlie Shibuk, Mike Nevins, among others. Let's just try to entertain each other and not feel we have to proselytize or justify our existence.

I enjoyed Guy's review of the Cooper-Clark book.

From John Reilly, 25 West St., Albany, NY 12206:

May I use a page of TMF to ask for readers' help? A colleague of mine at the State University of New York at Albany recently taught a course in Chemistry for non-science majors. To help develop principles of the field and of scientific method he asked students to read two detective novels in which knowledge of Chemistry is crucial: **Documents in the Case** and **Mysterious Affair at Styles**. He plans to offer the course again soon and would like to have suggestions for other readings. So, then, I ask for help. People may write to me, but I'm sure my friend would enjoy receiving mail directly from expert readers. if anyone wishes to help in this worthy effort they can write also to Professor John Aronson, Department of Chemistry, SUNY-Albany, Albany,

NY 12222.

From Barry Van Tilburg:

Apologies to Mr. Deeck and all the other spy fiction enthusiasts. Charlie did indeed abscond with the CIA funds besides making horses-asses of the British and American intelligence chiefs. Charlie's wife died saving Charlie's life in **Clap Hands Here Comes Charlie**. She was killed by Garson Ruttgers on page 189. The PBS show was great.

From Richard S. Callaghan, Jr.:

I see that we have at least a couple of top ten lists, so I thought that I would send in my check covering the prize and my list in an effort to win it back.
My top ten list is weakened by the fact that I'm a squirrel. I gleefully collect and put aside for future enjoyment what I expect to like best. My bomb shelter is stocked with some highly thought of Iles, Wades, and Highsmiths, all unread, which I would wager belong on my list, but after all, no one has read them all so here goes with what I have read, without excessive apology.

1-Christie, Agatha, **Five Little Pigs** (U.S. **Murder in Retrospect**) (1943) Her best--the perfect mystery.
2-Lovesey, Peter, **The False Inspector Dew** (1982) A hug yourself delight-A+.
3-Rendell, Ruth, **A Judgement in Stone** (1978) Superb writing--smooth, awesome inevitability.
4-Highsmith, Patricia, **The Talented Mr. Ripley** (1955) fascinating as a wounded snake.
5-Harling, Robert, **The Enormous Shadow** (1955) A gripping, believable spy yarn.
6-Berkeley, Anthony, **Jumping Jenny** (U.S. **Dead Mrs. Stratton**) (1933) A wicked put down--malicious.
7-Forester, C.S., **Payment Deferred** (1924) A kick in the guts)
8-McBain, Ed, **Guns** (1976) You'll care for a killer.
9-Clinton-Baddeley, V.C., **No Case for the Police** (1970) Sophisticated nostalgia—graceful and elegant.
10-Wade, Henry, **No Friendly Drop** (1931) Leisurely and memorable--good aftertaste.

Law school! If an old lawyer is any judge, I would think you are probably suited, Guy, but you might think twice before you take my opinion as a compliment. I do know that all of your readers wish you good luck and want to thank you for a job well done.

From Dick Schubert:

I can perhaps add something to Marvin Lachman's comment in 7:5 that the movie **Lady on a Train** was based on a Leslie Charteris story. In his introduction to the Bonded Mystery paperback **lady on a Train**, Charteris writes:

In the case of **Lady on a Train** we took the precaution of writing the picture first and the book afterwards.
The book also gives the following writing credits--
Original Screen story by Leslie Charteris

Screenplay by Edmund Beloin and Robert O'Brien
The cast listing includes Elizabeth Patterson (not Elisabeth Petterson) and Patricia Morison (not Morrison).

From Michael J. Tolley:

I was interested to read Joe R. Christopher's paper on "The Complexity of **The Nine Tailors**" in the July-August 83 issue. I have not read the secondary literature, so my additional remarks may have been anticipated but if not they may be of interest as a supplement to Joe's analysis.

The combination of Gothic horror and the theme of Providence or rather of divine justice employing various instruments to punish deacon and expose his crime relates Sayers' novel to many other works including the Elizabethan and Jacobean novellas collected under such titles as **The Triumphs of Gods Revenge Against...Murther** (John Reynolds, 1621-1635).

In such stories, it is important that no incident should appear on reflection, although not at first glance, to be accidental, in order that the theme of man's ignorance, blindness, deafness and stupidity (versus God's omniscience) might fully emerge. Thus it is important that the great detective, Wimsey, should often berate himself for these faults: God sees the truth instantly and, moreover, makes his witness plain, but man, supposedly intelligent, even when searching for the truth, may not only take months or years to recognize it but, in the end, must have it literally dinned into him (in the bell chamber), despite his having been one of the agents of justice, who literally know not what they do during the execution by bell-ringing on New Year's Eve. The related theme, of man's futile attempts to thwart justice by concealing the truth, evident in the use of disguise (Cranton's beard, Deacon's change of clothes and identities), is linked in a very interesting fashion to the leading idea of the bells as chief instruments of justice and exposure. (It is also a kind of change-ringing.) James Thoday's facial mutilation of Deacon suggests the hammer blows of the clappers of the bells which, like Deacon's corpse, applaud God without hands. That such a horrid pun is endemic to the spirit of the book may be judged by the rope business: Deacon is hanged, that is, judicially executed, through the bell rope that binds him, blindfolded by darkness, in a room with a long drop, through which of course hang the ropes pulled by ringers. (Cf. the quotation on hanging from Troyte which heads "The First Course".)

A fascinating aspect of the bells is their manner of articulating truth without words: they have tongues but are supposedly, ignorant, to be dumb, inanimate, mere noise-makers (on which cf. the opening remarks of Sayers' "Foreword"). Other witnesses in the novel are analogous to the bells, most conspicuously the Thodays' parrot and the village idiot, Potty Peake. The famous cipher fits here and it must be noticed that the parade of campanological learning really is essential to the plot of **The Nine Tailors**: you must understand campanology to solve the mystery, if you are, to use the appropriate metaphor, "hunting". Accordingly, the inattentive Mr. Venables anticipates Wimsey in solving the cipher, on which he promptly remarks, "simply", that "It was pure accident and due entirely to my failing vision". In this connexion, also, the importance of "tailors" may be found partly through the dumb testimony of Deacon's French underwear, which reveals an identity originally concealed by other clothings.

That the bells can somehow "see" the guilty person is felt by visitors to the bell-chamber, but the chief agent of vengeance is identified as Batty Thomas: bats, like God, can see in the dark. Batty Thomas, in the other sense of batty, links with the witness Potty Peake, who has "bats in the belfry". The "Thomas" part of the name identifies the bell (or stern Abbot who cast it) with doubting Wimsey, the detective who searches for tangible evidence. That the evidence concerns a kind of resurrected body has some theological force in the novel. The other unobserved witness, Cranton, also shows that even in the dark nothing goes unnoticed: Cranton hides in the belfry. However, the bells evoke a complex response: Wimsey says "they look as if they were going to come down on you:, a judicial image as well as one suggestive of entrapment. The cherubim on the ceiling repeat imagery of divine witness and mystery.

Readers more patient than myself will certainly find many other details in **The Nine Tailors** to reinforce these themes and images: they all go together to establish the work firmly as indeed a "complex novel". If we are to add one more category to the five or six discussed by Joe Christopher, we may like to see the novel as having a highly fashionable form, that of the metafiction: it is a detective fiction about the whole nature of detection and so of mystery fiction as a mirror to the combined mystery and revelation of the providential scheme in the Christian universe.

The function of the flood, with its heavy reminiscences of Genesis, may seem to stand somewhat apart from the central justice metaphor associated with the bells. It is, however, I submit, closely related to the central theme in this respect. Whereas the bells are concerned with justice at the individual level (and at this level the flood functions too in allowing the less sinful Will and Mary Thoday, excommunicated by adultery, to make atonement), the reference to Noah's flood invokes the idea of divine anger against a whole community of sinners. The disrepair of the sluice-gates is, in this reading, a metaphor for the modern disregard of old values. Several of the leading characters in the novel are found to impurely motivated, not merely the intrusive criminals and the visitor with her emeralds, Mrs. Wilbraham, who causes all the trouble in the first place, but even Mrs. Gates and Harry Gotobed (who drops coke on the church floor); on the other hand, it is amazing how many of the villagers are involved in the process of justice. Chief among them are the well-named Venables and it is not surprising that one of the Rector's most urgent duties at the time of the flood is baptism. Above all, against the flood, established by Providence for that purpose, stands the great church on its hill, an ark of refuge for the Christian village community, which is wonderfully united within its walls while the outward village, as it were, the buildings and the outhouses, the unconsecrated ground, is thoroughly sluiced by the great tide of waters.

GRISE NOTES: Obviously, this issue is four pages short. For the longest time I couldn't figure out how that could have happened, but it came to me in an embarrassing flash of light--the edit disk I sent to Steve contained the old TMF parameters, and I had modified those parameters slightly on my machine. The result is that my machine squeezed Steve's fifty pages into forty-six. We'll work it out before next time.

I had not intended to write anything for or in this issue, but since I had to append the above note explaining the missing four pages, I might as well blither along for a while and fill up some of the unsightly white spaces that remain in this malnourished issue. I should remark at the outset that I have not read any of the copy herein, and I am looking forward, after all the printing, collating, stapling, and envelope-stuffing are done, to sitting down with a copy and reading it from cover to cover, with it all being fresh material, not stuff that I have worked on for hours at the keyboard before it ever shows up in

www.ingramcontent.com/pod-product-compliance
Lightning Source LLC
Chambersburg PA
CBHW031437040426
42444CB00006B/848